THE ICONS WITHIN

THE ICONS WITHIN

Iconic Therapy and the Healing
Journey to Personal Freedom

GEORGE PUGH, Ph.D.

THE ICONS WITHIN
ICONIC THERAPY AND THE HEALING
JOURNEY TO PERSONAL FREEDOM

iUniverse books may be ordered through booksellers or by contacting:

iUniverse
1663 Liberty Drive
Bloomington, IN 47403
www.iuniverse.com
1-800-Authors (1-800-288-4677)

ISBN: 978-1-4917-6739-9 (sc)
ISBN: 978-1-4917-6740-5 (hc)
ISBN: 978-1-4917-6741-2 (e)

Library of Congress Control Number: 2015907103

Print information available on the last page.

iUniverse rev. date: 5/16/2016

This book is dedicated to those who after reading it, take on the tough journey to free themselves from the Icons that once kept them safe and vigilant but now discourage their movement forward.

This book is also dedicated to my wife Christine. Thanks for your editing, mentoring, and loving support. I could not have done it without you.

The Reader's Journey

Preface

Over the years as a psychologist I have come to an understanding of how the personality forms and why, quite often, that formation is counterproductive to healthy functioning. In the early years of my career I tried, with some but not enough success, to point out to my clients their very obvious errors in thinking that contributed to the various psychological symptoms they manifested, symptoms characteristic and typical of a personality that just did not work. They were chronically depressed or quick to anger, overly anxious or overwhelmed with doubt. When I worked with the criminal population I would see the same patterns only in more extreme forms. I discovered and developed some basic therapeutic interventions or exercises that, if completed by the client, consistently allowed them to change for the better. This book will explain how you can break free of old patterns of behavior that simply do not work for you. Unfortunately, it is not the easiest of journeys.

As you read this book you will come to know that there is often an intensity during the therapeutic journey that indicates that progress is being made. This level of intensity might startle you. I had a number of editors review what I had written. One suggested that the book had too quick a start. It was too intense too soon. I realized this was true, so I made some changes to soften the beginning. She also wrote the following, which I believe may be a way of addressing her concern and easing you, the reader, into the journey ahead.

> In *The Icons Within: Iconic Therapy and the Healing Journey to Personal Freedom,* you will be given a ticket, which you may choose to use at any time to get on and off the train to your past. The engineer will stop at the stations that you wish to visit. The conductor will guide you through the countryside, busy cities, and sometimes very dark tunnels. You can sit back and just watch as the scenery goes by, or you can choose to pull the cord, stop the train, recall memories from that station, address the baggage that you find on the platform, and, finally, discard the control much of it has over you. There may be several stops, and some may be very frightening. As the train slows, you may even become paralyzed, but your courage will support your yearning to climb down to the platform, go to the stationmaster, and speak those words you may have rehearsed for years. Leaving the baggage there and addressing the label to the correct recipient will be a joyous occasion. As the whistle blows and the steam powers your engine to now move into the future, you will recognize a surge of delight and a tour of the grand life you have chosen.
>
> —Lee Hewitt, June 2012

Another editor, read a version of the book that had at the end a storage section for the written work of clients who had taken part in the program. (The treatment program includes a number of optional writing exercises for the clients.) What the clients had written was often powerful. I had typed and stored their written work for later use. Out of kindness and concern for others, these clients gave permission for their written work to be used in this book with the hope that the readers might find some comfort in knowing that they were not alone with their suffering.

It was not my plan to use their written work extensively but rather as examples of the key concepts that underlie this approach to healing. This editor insisted on reading all of the clients' written material. She informed me that she had found herself rushing from one chapter to the next to get to the quotes from the actual clients. As well, she had read all of the quotations stored at the end. As a result, I realized that what these clients had to say as advocates for healing was, for her, as important as a description of the healing process. So I have included a significant number of the writings of program participants, with identifying features altered to ensure privacy. Here is the first sample.

> *I came into this program very scared. I felt very alone. I didn't believe I had a voice. I didn't trust anyone—least of all myself. I didn't know how to let anyone in. In my eyes, I was lost, with almost no hope. Dr. Pugh kept talking about doing the steps in the program. He believed I would feel a certain freedom by doing them. My first disclosure was hard, but I survived without anything bad happening to me. It's a good thing I had no writing to do. I shook pretty bad for a while.*[1]

---

[1] Identifying features regarding clients have been changed to protect their privacy.

Before We Begin, Some Cautions

I know how it feels to be betrayed and abused and to have to fear the future. I know how it feels to believe that what is inside of you is nothing but evil and hatred. I know how it is to spit poison and feel the boiling blood course through your body.

As a psychologist for over 30 years, I have worked with clients from every walk of life; teachers, priests, housewives, prisoners, tradesmen, and business executives. They have presented with a variety of problems, including serious psychological disorders, relationship concerns and feelings of depression and anxiety. For the most part all of them carried powerful self-condemning thoughts of worthlessness. Their fears and anxieties were often triggered by the challenges of daily life. I began to notice consistencies and commonalities in these clients that were seldom mentioned in the theories on psychology that had served as the underpinnings for my training. I began to break free from the limitations of the treatment processes I had been taught. Then, when I was contracted to offer a therapy program in a prison setting, the basic principles of Iconic therapy began to form in my mind.

For years during therapy sessions, especially with very troubled individuals, I sensed an inner negative energy. I could feel, sometimes only for brief moments, that energy emanating from them. I realized that energy came from the heart of their problems. With therapeutic discussion, we could expose the source of this reverberating negative energy and then together, we could come to an understanding of the problem and its various dimensions. The source and the cause of the negative energy needed to be understood and that negative energy needed to be released. There was a battle within. Somehow, one part of the *self* was fighting with and condemning another part of the *self* with this negative energy. This negative energy, with its self-condemning qualities, could hide within and even disappear temporarily after it had been exposed and the nature of its existence challenged in therapy sessions. Often hours of conventional talk therapy were spent understanding where that negative energy had come from. Discussions continued with the conviction that there was no longer a need for the presence of this negative energy. However, even after lengthy talk therapy sessions, that negative energy would often return in the form of anxiety, discouragement, resentment, and anger. Often the client would conclude that nothing was ever going to change.

I also began to notice that a constant, yet subtle, hunger for safety and escape from the negative energy was present within these clients. That need for safety included an unhealthy longing for secrecy and distraction. If they somehow could get to that place in their minds where, even for a moment, they did not think about the problems of the past, then they might find a modicum of tranquility. I realized that this longing for safety, secrecy, and sanctuary had become strong enough to hold them back, not only from the changes that were necessary for healing but also from healthy risk-taking in general. As a result, their journeys in life often led to places of refuge that were safe, but stagnant, to destinations they had not truly wanted, to small comforts that were just enough to settle them but never enough to allow a sense of fulfillment or connection with the essence of life. They soon came to know, after brief moments of relief in these places of safety, that the negative energy would return to generate self-condemning thoughts and feelings that constantly discouraged and frustrated them.

I now know that virtually everyone carries negative energy in the form of unexpressed, unspoken, never-shared memories of pain, suffering, sadness and frustration for much longer than necessary. Many pretend that the painful memories have faded, although they remain as fresh as yesterday. Far too many presume that if they have physically survived their history of injustice, then that is enough. Many conclude that the psychological damage of the past is inconsequential and will fade with time. It will not.

I believe that this is a basic characteristic of the human condition. The pain and suffering of the past cause us to shape our personalities to protect ourselves. These self-defending strategies succeed, but leave us overly guarded against the reoccurrence of similar pain, suffering, and trauma. It is part of a life-altering process that affects all of us. I discovered the harshest truth of all. The secrets of past and recent injustices leave a residue of shame, anxiety, resentment, and self-condemnation that will slow, interfere with, or stop our journey to actualize our true selves.

Ahead are the directions for the healing journey developed to remove this negative energy from within. You may find it difficult to read about the strategies and the examples cited. It may be even more difficult to put these healing strategies into action. This book is similar to a series of therapy sessions in which you will be able to consider exercises that will change your life. You will read about clients who were encouraged to speak thoughts and express emotions never before revealed. Some of the problems shared will remind you of your own concerns and may be very difficult to read. They may even bring tears.

If along the way a paragraph is too difficult to get through, put the book down. You will have encountered the anxiety within that keeps you safe but holds you back from where you want to go. Reading about a truth that you do not want to face may trigger feelings of anxiety. The strategies in this book will teach you how to not only take charge of this anxiety but to eliminate it or at least shrink it. These therapeutic interventions will show you how to accept and embrace the truth about who you were and who you have become. Remember you, not your anxiety and not your anger, are the captain of your ship. Take a break from the reading when you feel that need. Breathe and let your anxiety recede. Remind yourself that this is *your journey* and you can set *your own pace.*

Psychological change is a gradual and sometimes painful process. The strategies in this book will allow you to eventually gain control and overcome your sadness, anxiety, fear, and anger. Victory is ahead if you want it, but resistance, denial, self-doubt and sadness may get in the way. Please know that some of these paragraphs brought sadness and tears to me, so it is okay for you to have a tear or two as well.

I would like to be your guide but I will only do so with your permission. If the road gets rocky, take a rest. If excessive anxiety is triggered by something you read, take that paragraph to your psychologist[2] or therapist and read it together. Bring in a support team. You will learn that you no longer need your anxiety to protect you from injustices long-since passed. The healing journey ahead is difficult but it is worth it. It will be scary, but it will also be liberating. I will wait for you in the pages ahead.

Here is one woman calling for you to begin your healing journey. Even though it may sound a little intimidating, you know that she has tasted victory. *You* can too.

> *My name is … and I need all the women, men, and children that suffer from any kind of abuse to stand up and know that the shame is not yours. You don't deserve it; you never did. We were never born to be at the mercy of abuse. We have suffered more than enough, and it's time to take a stand and be strong and fight for our rights … to break free from all the hurt and torment we went through and no longer feel the pain and guilt, to free our hearts of shame and no longer carry that anymore.*
>
> *We are beautiful and strong. We need to use the gift of courage that we have to set us free.*

---

[2] I have used the terms *psychologist, psychiatrist, counsellor,* and *therapist* interchangeably, as most with the appropriate training will be able to use the Iconic approach.

CHAPTER 1
The Icons³ Within

Are you living a life that just does not feel right? Have you thought about seeing a psychologist, psychiatrist or counsellor but do not have the time, energy, or courage to turn and face the unsettling reality of your life, a life you believe is less than what it could be? Often it is difficult to see a psychologist, psychiatrist or counsellor, as you feel embarrassed that you have a problem you cannot solve and you have to seek help from a stranger. Sometimes you are ashamed of a hidden past about which you have never spoken but which you know is in the way. Often you are depressed and discouraged. Life itself is dragging you down.

If you find yourself secretly nodding yes to these comments, then please know that this book is written with you in mind. There is a way out, a means for you to find release from whatever it is that holds you back. There is a way to achieve inner clarity and a mindset that is energized and optimistic, with a passion for going forward that is so strong that you will forget about those thoughts of giving up. Here, one of my clients describes her efforts to acknowledge and

---

³ I have capitalized the word *Icon* and its derivatives to indicate that this concept, as explained in this theory, is unique and holds psychological meaning beyond the conventional use of the term.

release her sense of anger and injustice regarding problems from her past:

> *What happened to me made me feel a lot of shame and worthlessness. The memories have haunted me for the past 16 years and have caused me nothing but pain and trouble. It is time to end this pain I feel ... I am tired of keeping this pressed down inside of me. It hurts too much. I have enough pain in my life that I have caused myself to deal with; it's time for this to come out. I am not hiding this pain anymore; it hurts too much, and all the anger this has caused for me, I don't need anymore.*

If you sincerely attempt the strategies that are described in this book, I believe you will begin to experience significant changes in the way you see the world and yourself. You will move beyond the pain and suffering from past hurts and indignities. You will sense a lasting change within and a deeper sense of personal integrity. I have witnessed this approach work time and time again having used these strategies successfully with over 500 clients. Although this process is emotionally painful, it is very powerful. If you are willing to risk brief emotional upheaval and painful moments of reflection, combined with tears, you will find that you have moved forward through your healing to discover and release your true self.

Something Is Not Quite Right

Right now, in this moment, you know or at least suspect that there is something wrong. There is something within that prevents you from leading the life you desire: a life with passion, commitment, and self-confidence. Sometimes, like the person quoted above, you have an idea of what it is that holds you back from this more powerful connection with life itself. Possibly you have never said it out loud to another person. You might even believe that if you share some unsettling aspect of your past, this might be the starting point for change.

You give it some thought and decide that possibly a discussion with a professional or even a trusted friend would lead to some insight and the changes you want—if you could only find the courage to take that step. On the other hand, you may decide to travel silently and privately, at least in the beginning, by reading this book. That is a positive step too.

If you are travelling alone, I ask you to observe others engaging in the treatment process I will describe below and then imagine that you are following the therapeutic strategies recommended. In your mind, begin to acknowledge your hidden problems. This is the first step required for change. This effort can be very positive. Unfortunately, these efforts can also be unsettling. Do not be afraid if you begin to feel upset. That is part of the journey. Eventually, when you are brave enough, you may throw caution aside and pick a psychologist, psychiatrist, therapist, or counsellor and, within the privacy and confidentiality offered, attempt to change. For now, read along as I describe how Iconic therapy was developed, and follow the participants who took part in the powerful therapeutic strategies which brought lasting and positive change to their lives.

▶ The first step

You will discover that the psychologist, psychiatrist, therapist, or counsellor that you choose first tries to develop a relationship of trust with you. He or she tries to present a sense of safety and a place where you can share your problems. You find an accepting and secure relationship from which to launch your search for a more passionate and involved version of yourself. Finally, the unspeakable is spoken. You share a secret that has haunted you and may possibly have been holding you back. You experience a sense of relief.

Once this breakthrough has occurred, the discussion of the problem begins in earnest. Good progress seems to be made. You feel better for a while, but then the same nagging anxiety, the same frustration, the same emptiness returns. The treatment sessions begin to lose their impact. You find yourself at a loss for what to do next. What should follow the tenth or eleventh session, after the conversations have circled the problem and examined its every dimension? From this point on, the direction of each session is often left to you. Both you and the counsellor have found that talking about the problem brings some relief. With the problem revealed, you consider strategies for change, agree to them, and attempt them. You understand your issues more clearly and yet the anxiety remains.

▶ Is the counseling enough?

Even with the insight you have acquired, the effort to change seems to go against the grain of your personality. It is as if you have been brainwashed to continue to act and, more specifically, feel as you always have. After the initial experience of relief, the progress that resulted from the first series of sessions with a psychologist or counsellor only comes in small doses. Change seems only temporary. It is as if you and the therapist, like Sisyphus of Greek mythology, are pushing that rock up a hill together. When you reach what appears to be the top, you have some answers and some understanding, but no lasting inner change. You eventually realize that there is a mountain-climb of joyless existence still ahead. In one moment of weakness, that rock, that burden of anxiety and discouragement, rolls back to the bottom. You fall into your old ways of being, left to start again, more knowledgeable but more weary and resigned than before. You may think that nothing will ever really change.

A New Theory on How to Change Your Personality

I strongly believe there is hope for you even if the counselling that you tried (or considered) did not work (or did not impress) as thoroughly as you might have wanted. The new theory I have developed and tested presumes that the problem or problems that you suffer from have at their foundation an almost unalterable mindset. Most likely you have developed a style of thinking and processing your concerns that appear (to you) to be the *only* way to think and feel about your experiences. The way you have been processing information and solving problems is programmed within you; it has been established to maintain and improve your survivability. That is why you are so reluctant to change. Your survival-oriented way of perceiving your problem and further, your way of perceiving the world in general, is part of the problem. It is so solidly in place that it is almost impossible, to change. Talking with a counsellor about your problems and how you might solve them is helpful. However, even with the therapeutic efforts at talking through and understanding your problems, the negative way you feel about yourself as a person often remains.

▶ New discoveries made with those who have suffered extreme trauma

Many of the discoveries underlying this theory were made in prison settings. While working in a number of different prisons, I found that the inmates arrived with problems similar to those clients I treated in the community. The only difference was that problems of the incarcerated clients were greater in number and severity than those of their community counterparts and often originated from a multitude of powerful and deeply traumatic sources. For some, but certainly not all, their recent incarceration triggered a strong interest in and commitment to change. They had been forcibly removed from the environment that had led them, and continually tempted them, to take part in criminal behavior. In part, imprisonment forced them to stop what they had been doing and asked them to take a long and serious look at their lives. It was similar to the ashram experience that law-abiding citizens sometimes choose in order to spend time on reflection, hoping to find a better way to live their lives.

These prisoners were similar to you or me. They wanted change, and they wanted it badly. Some were willing to take risks that many of us would prefer to avoid: risks in the form of difficult therapeutic interventions that I presented to them.

At times, I would only have a few sessions with these inmates. Given the pressure of the circumstances, individual time spent per session was generally less than ideal; often only a few half-hour sessions could be arranged. This resulted in strategies that quickly focused on the core of the problem and then a direct attack on that problem. Significant inner changes began to occur that impacted the basic organization of the personality, especially those aspects responsible for perceiving and processing problems. By tolerating and overcoming the anxiety and self-doubt that blocked personal growth, these clients were able to discover and release more authentic versions of who they really were.

I then began to use and develop these strategies in a group format for imprisoned women who had suffered every variation of trauma one could imagine: physical, emotional, sexual, and psychological. It became evident that the impact of the group and the support of the other group members magnified the power and efficiency of these strategies. A description of that program will reveal the basic principles for personal growth that can be used to address all types of problems. I found that these strategies worked for men and women who were living their lives well below their potential, living with secrets that haunted them and discouragement that held them back.

These extremely dysfunctional individuals, who had had to be imprisoned to find a semblance of stability and sobriety, found healing in both small and large doses through the strategies I presented to them. When they entered the program, they were functioning in the bottom third of the adult population. Upon successfully completing these therapeutic interventions, they had achieved the potential to move to the middle third of the population. Some of them were able to become law abiding citizens who were respectful of the rights of others.

▶ The same strategies can be applied to your problems

The same strategies can be used for the average person, a person similar to you. With these interventions, you can move to a higher level after finding release from the inner conflicts with which you struggle. If you take part in this healing journey you will begin to feel stronger in your efforts to fulfill the responsibilities of daily living. With the successful completion of the strategies developed in this program, you will slowly evolve to become a person not easily threatened by the hurtful comments of others. You will begin to experience a sense of peacefulness within. You will be more often touched by moments of joyfulness in living a life with direction. You will be able to more clearly perceive the problems of daily life and then actualize well-reasoned solutions. Finally, and most importantly, you will find your true voice.

CHAPTER 2
The Formation and Shaping of the Personality

Remembering Mom

When I try to remember you, in the past,
Is something I don't want to last,
But all I can really see clear
Is you with that crack pipe.
I would never have thought as a kid
My own mom would be the type.

I used to lie for you,
So we could try to stay together
For whatever weather.

I also try to stay brave
In hope you can be saved,
When I cry and cry, the tears make my eyes swell
And back then and even now
I feel that I am in my own hell.

You used to beat me and pull it off discreet. You teased me then and now.
Is it to please yourself, or does it make you feel big and strong?

I didn't do anything wrong to you but love you,
And that is true.

All I wanted was to be with you and to change stage by stage.
That is what I wanted all my life …
I look to the blue sky; I wish I could fly;
I don't care for me or anyone anymore,
So the tears pour, and I fail like I knew I would one day.

—The betrayed son

One thing you will notice when you take part in Iconic therapy is your resistance to some or all of the exercises. Your resistance is to be expected, as you will be asked to change the way you process and understand your problem and your relationship with it. That may feel uncomfortable and unnatural and lead to your reluctance to engage in the treatment exercises. In one sense, you have the problem, and then you have your way of coping with the problem. Unfortunately, it adds up to two problems. The second problem, your coping strategies, is best understood in terms of the principles of survival, which are the underpinnings of Iconic therapy.

Survival Is the Basic Need

When you were first born, you held within a tremendous energy and longing to connect with your mother. You needed your mother for your survival. If the situation was ideal, you made that connection. Your mother loved you and fulfilled your needs for nurturing and growth. Ideally, she was there for you when you were completely dependent and vulnerable. She was essential for your survival.

However, no mother is perfect. The conditions for your growth and care were, most likely, less than ideal. As an infant, you reacted instinctively to any threat to your survival. Anytime your mother was angry or upset with you, your infant self would interpret that as a threat to your survival. You would adjust your behavior to maximize your chances for survival. These adaptive reactions set the stage for the development of your personality.

▶ Threats to survival are stored at the core of the personality

Threats to survival reside at the core of the personality structure. These threatening events often occur during youth. Even though extreme examples will be used to explain this theory of how the personality forms, the reader is reminded that even less-extreme threats to survival will lead to the same process and similarly shape and alter the formation of the personality.

Let us begin with a young person who has suffered, like the young person who wrote the rap poem at the beginning of this chapter. As a child he perceived a life-threatening event or series of events that he understood as not only threatening but unfair. Let us say, for the sake of a clarifying example, that this person's mother repeatedly threatened to abandon him. This had a powerful impact on his developing *personality*, which was then shaped and altered to protect his true self.

▶ The personality forms to protect the true self

In the formative stages, the personality adjusts in order to deal directly with perceived life-threatening events. All of us have endured life-threatening or integrity-threatening events. Because survival is the most important need, simple and primitive strategies that improve our chances for survival become hardwired into the brain. This has allowed us to survive not only the initial threat but also to prepare for a possible reoccurrence of that threat. In other words, all of us put in place personalized emergency strategies to avoid or minimize potentially life-threatening circumstances that may occur again in the future. The perception of the world as an unsafe and ominous place begins to form. We become more careful and vigilant. Our fears and anxieties are now triggered by certain threatening elements in our environment. Our personality forms in a manner to avoid these feared elements. Specialized strategies are now put in place within the personality to protect the true self.

Icons Represent Life-Threatening Events

The threatening events (or ongoing, unfair threatening situations), whether mild or severe, are stored in our memories in symbolic form. For example, the stored image of the mother, father, or a stranger, perpetrating life-threatening behaviors on a young person can be deeply engrained in memory. To survive these traumatic or upsetting events, the young person cannot, at the time, express all of his or her feelings—especially disappointment, frustration, and anger—as this expression could increase the threat to survival. These feeling left unexpressed externally, reverberate within building upon themselves and leaving the person often quite anxious, confused, angry and frustrated.

As human beings are a cognitive species, these unexpressed emotions are processed and interpreted with thoughts and conclusions that, at one level, seek to explain their existence. However, these supporting cognitive processes are also subjected to survival forces and one's cognitive understanding of their fears and anxieties are thus oriented to enhance survival and avoid pain, suffering, and threats of death. Just as the attached unexpressed emotion—held back to maintain safety—can at times reach out-of-control proportions in the form of anxiety and related emotions, the cognitions as well, because they are primarily internal, can be mentally re-processed many times in an effort to understand what is occurring and in that effort build a mindset that is cognitively compatible with survival strategies but replete with errors in thinking.

I have used the term *Icon* to represent the memory and the attached mental imagery of the threatening experience and its energy that is stored in the personality. The term Icon depicts a powerful symbol and a pervasive omnipresence. Historically, the term is often used to represent pictures and images of religious figures, such as Jesus, Buddha, and the devil. The Icons within one's mind are perceived as having this type of power and presence. The mother described in the poem at the opening of this chapter represents a strong Icon within the son's personality. The mother's symbolic omnipresence in his mind continually reminds this young man of her rejection.

The term Icon in everyday life is also used to describe the symbols on a computer monitor, where one click leads to a program of images and strategies. The Icons within the personality are similar, in that one triggering word, sensation, or event in the perception of the person clicks into consciousness the frightening or rejecting images stored within (like the rejecting mother).

Attached to the frightening Icon are prominent sensations that were present and noticed during those times of threat: smells, colors, patterns, sounds, music, places, houses, rooms, people, voices, etc. When these reoccur in everyday life, long after the threatening experiences have ended, feelings of unexpressed anger and frustration come to the surface, accompanied by uneasiness, anxiety, fear, and sadness. Memories, partial or whole, of the threatening or traumatic experience from the past are brought to the forefront of consciousness and the mind prepares for the possibility that a threatening situation might manifest. Sometimes the frightening Icon itself takes a central place in the focus of the personality. During these warning stages, cognitive strategies to address and prepare for life-threatening danger are considered and the direction of one's behavior is oriented to seek out places and feelings of safety and survival.

We all hold Icons, both positive and negative, within. As the basement rests on the footings below, the foundation of the personality rests on these Icons. When the Icon is negative, it affects the entire structure above, weakening it. For most of us, the negative Icons are not too extreme—yet they still carry negative energy that interferes with our striving to become all that we can. For some of us, the Icons are extremely negative and carry powerful counterproductive forces that interfere with personal development.

▶ An example of threat to one's existence

Let us imagine that you endured extreme abuse as a child that threatened your existence. As this approach works for all types of abuse, when the term *abuse* is used below, substitute for that one word one of the following descriptors that fits your experiences: *sexual abuse*, *physical abuse*, or *psychological/verbal abuse*. All abuse shapes the personality in some manner.

▶ Survival strategies are personalized and kept secret

When you suffer abuse and unfairness, especially as a young person, you feel threatened and become concerned that your survival is at risk. The person abusing you generally justifies their actions and lets you know—sometimes directly, sometimes indirectly (i.e., with abusive actions, words, and assumptions)—that you deserved this abuse. You are told, or it is implied, that you are not worthy of the respect and love that others experience. Since the abuse may be all that you have known in your limited life experience, to improve your chances for survival in this threatening situation, you agree with the abuser. You try to "be good" for the abusive person to console him and make him[4] less threatening. To improve your chances for survival even further, you personalize the perpetrator's message and cognitively make it your own: "You are right; I do deserve the abuse. I am unworthy. I will try harder." Your survival strategies and thought patterns reach the stage where they are triggered automatically in certain stressful situations, like a reflex: "I deserved it; I'm just not worthy; I'm not like

---

[4] For the sake of simplicity, the abuser is presumed in this example to be a male. Of course, both males and females can be abusive.

everyone else; I am less than others." Unfortunately, even when you are physically removed from the dangerous situation, you still carry these demeaning cognitions. These cognitions were part of the survival strategies that worked in the limited environment where you were being abused. However, they are counterproductive in other non-threatening situations, and often they interfere with your daily interactions, adding unnecessary mental chaos and confusion to your life.

These demeaning and personalized destructive thoughts are repeated mentally over and over as reminders to keep you aligned with safe strategies. They find a place in the foundation of your personality. While you feel a little safer with this survival approach, at a deeper level you become increasingly convinced that you are unworthy. Furthermore, you instinctively keep both your unworthiness and the abuse secret. You conclude that it is best to keep your situation—whether physical abuse, sexual abuse, parental neglect, or some other form of abuse—secret. From your perspective, to reveal these circumstances threatens your existence even more.

In This Process, the Icon Forms

The stored mental imagery of the abuser and the abuse that you have endured are held within your mind. This stored mental imagery, the Icon, feeds on the survival energy available within your personality. When triggered—for example, when the menacing perpetrator returns to the environment or when his tone of voice changes— the stored imagery sends warning messages. This symbol within, the Icon, and the resultant highly charged response to the symbol, become energized mental forces. At first, these inner forces are functional in promoting survival. Later, these forces may rage out of control and trigger a variety of mental health problems, including anxiety, depression, rigidity, inflexibility, and in extreme cases, psychic paralysis. These symptoms form the basis for a variety of personality disorders.

The Icons Initially Increase the Chances of Survival

This mental entity, with its often fear-related imagery, sensations and cognitions, represents a life-threatening/life-altering energized memory that easily triggers survival reactions. This Icon, the stored mental symbol, personifies the abuser and the abusive situation. It found its place within your personality so that your chances for survival and safety would be enhanced. For example, when you sense danger, you are perceiving an event or a circumstance that has a similarity to an upsetting or dangerous memory from your past. The Icon that represents this ominous memory and the feelings associated with the Icon (especially anxiety) are brought into consciousness. You then, reflexively activate survival strategies that were successful in the past in the form of feelings, behaviors, and mental dialogue. This same Icon has the potential to influence you throughout your life.

In summary, these forces within, these negative Icons, have two purposes: first, to remind you of impending danger in the environment and, second, to trigger survival strategies and ways of coping. You develop a multitude of protective strategies to ensure survival when elements in your environment are perceived as potentially threatening.

The Iconic Echo

When an Icon forms, it creates an Iconic echo which begins to reverberate. The Iconic echo is the mental energy expressed as an echo of thoughts and feelings emanating from the Icon that remind you of past trauma/injustice. The echo is triggered into consciousness when you perceive trauma-related dangers ahead. The purpose of the echo is to encourage caution, vigilance and survival-related reactions. Sometimes the echo is experienced as a voice within, speaking to you from the perspective of the perpetrator, telling you that you deserved the abuses of the past. At other times the echo is more diffuse and is experienced as a wave of anxiety that comes over you with little or no conscious connection to previously experienced trauma.

The Iconic echo continually reverberates throughout your personality and, although it is initially supportive of survival, it eventually contaminates your efforts for personal growth and development. In the end, the Icon, with its devastating Iconic echo, has the power to destroy the essence of personhood. Often the negative Iconic echo ("You're not worthy"), initially put in place to keep you safe, is heard for a life time. It is a powerful negative force that distracts you from your efforts to find success, happiness, and fulfillment. It encourages you to remain with careful and vigilant survival strategies in order to avoid dangers that are no longer present.

The Iconic Reaction

The Iconic reaction is the actualization of your self-condemning thoughts. These are the strategies required to be consistent with the Iconic echo. The Iconic reaction begins with the personalization of the Iconic echo. "You're not worthy" becomes "I'm not worthy." It is often takes on the characteristics of compliance: "I will take action to comply with the abuser; I will agree with him, I am not worthy. This opinion will keep me safe." As well, compliance generally develops an underlying layer of contrasting emotions; deep and abiding feelings of anger, hatred, and shame: "I hate always complying. I am angry for being in this mess. I hate myself for being part of that. I'm getting lost in my hatred for what happened to me. Sometimes, I hate myself."

▶ The tertiary Iconic reaction

Compliance coping strategies ("I agree I am not worthy") followed by self-loathing ("I hate myself for not being worthy") lead to a third and often very destructive phase, addiction ("I'll get drunk because I cannot live with myself and my history"). Your self-loathing thoughts, which are often consistent with how your abuser thought about you, are at times overwhelming. To avoid and numb these feelings you turn to the comforts of addiction and self-abuse. ("When I hurt too much, it is okay to drink too much. He disrespects me, and I guess I disrespect me.")

▶ Healthy risk-taking is compromised

The personality,[5] in its efforts to perceive and process injustice, abuse and trauma, initially places the Icon in the forefront of consciousness, especially when you are under stress. The personality then begins to create consistent and complementary survival strategies: the Iconic echo and the Iconic reaction. An unfortunate, long-term, and devastating side effect of these protective strategies is an aversion to any thought or behavior that would further risk survival. In fact, these "keep-safe" coping strategies serve to contaminate and conflict with natural tendencies for healthy risk-taking and interfere with the true self's[6] interest in exploring the environment and rising to the everyday challenges of general growth and fulfillment. When it is time to stop and think about planning your personal development, you will struggle because you have been conditioned to believe that your life and your integrity are at risk or perceived to be at risk. You cannot give full attention to achieving personal growth and fulfillment when you constantly feel a need to find safety and security.

The negative Icon, the echo of its voice and image, and your fear reaction, all improved your chances of living through life-threatening

---

[5] The term *personality* in this theory is used to describe those strategies, behaviors, thoughts, and feelings developed to first protect the true self (by choosing survival strategies) and second (when one's survival is well-established) to encourage the true self to find higher levels of expression.

[6] The "true self" is the essence of the person, his or her true nature.

trauma because they continually reminded you of potential dangers ahead. Even after surviving the trauma, the presence of the Icon constantly reminds you that the trauma may return. Anything in the environment similar to elements of the earlier trauma, the sights, sounds, smells, textures, and tastes can bring back horrible memories from the past and poison any thought of a future where you can find clarity and justice. These reminders will trigger the Iconic echo: the thought that you are not worthy of anything but survival.

These reflexive actions, which include fear, anxiety, and anger, become part of the foundation of your personality and prevent you from developing a full life. Even reading this book may remind you of what you endured and may increase your anxiety level to the point where you feel discouraged about reading further. Nevertheless, I encourage you to read on. The more you examine your problems realistically, the better prepared you will be to deal with the Icons within.

The Problems We Inherit

We all hold negative Icons within to a certain extent. Unfortunately, when the person who abused you or treated you unfairly has left the scene, or the events that hurt you so much have long since ended, you still remain bound to the strategies that allowed you to survive those difficult moments of your past. You became an expert at living within your dysfunctional environment while at the same time you remain confused and lost in the real world beyond. When it comes to changing strategies to adjust to the evolving challenges of your personal journey towards growth and development, you are stuck. You have become committed to thoughts, behaviors, and strategies that were designed for survival in wartime conditions, but the war is over.

The Challenge We Are Given

All of us unknowingly live in accordance with deeply ingrained strategies, thought patterns, and emotional reactions that at one time were essential but are now counterproductive to our growth and fulfillment. This is the nature of the human condition. The secret to personal success and inner freedom is first to understand the abusive and life-altering experiences we have endured and the resulting negative Icons that have found a place within our personalities. We need to understand that it is these negative Icons that bind our thoughts and feelings to fears emanating from past abuse and that these same Icons hold us to the erroneous conclusion that we deserved the abuse we endured. Then we need to realize that there are strategies that we can use to remove these negative forces within from their positions of power. That is your challenge—to stop reflexively using survival strategies that are counterproductive and in their place actualize strategies that will eliminate or at least significantly reduce the power of the negative Icons within.

To this point I have isolated the problematic Icons to those that developed during the early years of your history, when you were a child or teenager. However, the same principles apply to traumatic experiences endured during adulthood. These include the loss of loved ones, especially those lost as a consequence of murder or suicide. Such events can also lead to the development of an Iconic presence. The mental presence of the lost loved one finds a place within the personality. Iconic echoes begin to resonate with unexpressed feelings, which often include anger, sadness, frustration, and confusion. If we want to live full lives, we must be able to move beyond the injustices of the past and not allow ourselves to be defined entirely or even partially by the negative and hurtful aspects of our history. We must take control of our own lives and define ourselves.

CHAPTER 3
The Nature of Humanity

I ran away from home because my mom always physically and mentally abused me. Since I can remember, she hit me, told me that she didn't love me, and wished she never had me ... I remember one time my mom and I got into one of our biggest fights. I lied about having my homework done when I didn't. I remember her yelling, and I flinched because I thought she was going to hit me. She always made me flinch. Then she started yelling louder, "Why are you moving? Do you think I am going to hit you?" It's how it always started. It's like she became someone else when she'd hit me, I would always leave in my head, go somewhere other than being there right then. She made me sleep in the hallway that night (why, I don't know). That night I cried myself to sleep, always wondering what I did to make her hate me so much. In the morning, I packed my school bag with some clothes, all the money I had for a 13-year-old, and the lighter and smokes I stole from my uncle. I told my sisters how much I loved them and that no matter what happened it was never their fault. I couldn't tell them that after school I was going to run away, because they always made me promise I wouldn't go. I left school in the afternoon and walked

*down to Smyth street, all the way down to … I was crying
a lot, thinking, what am I going to do? It was cold out
because it was the beginning of winter. Because of the cold,
I decided to sleep in the park. I was walking through the
parking lot when someone grabbed me and threw me on
top of a parked car. All I could really remember from that
moment was how cold the car felt on my back. When he
finished, he spit on me and just left me there. That was the
first time I ever had "sex" and the last time I ever talked
about it till I was 18.*

The Human Condition Is Filled with Limiting Icons

We are all raised by individuals who, like us, have flaws. They may have related to us in a manner that threatened our existence. We responded with survival strategies that eventually interfered with our efforts to achieve a life filled with passion, purpose, and accomplishment. Further, as we proceeded into adulthood, many of us were visited by other, very upsetting, life-altering events. These, too, may had led to the installation of survival strategies to get us through—but left us almost unable to go to the next stage in life.

The purpose of the terminology used in Iconic therapy is to explain why we continually make life choices that hold us back from taking healthy risks. When we use this terminology to conceptualize development, we can find a way out of the abyss of hurt feelings endured and irrational decisions too frequently taken. Let us begin by looking at the steps we can take toward changing the flaws in the foundations of our personalities. Let us begin *the healing journey.*

Iconic Therapy

▶ Undoing the power of the Icons

Strategies to find freedom and inner peace

The basic underpinnings of Iconic therapy were developed in a group-therapy program for imprisoned women, who had suffered the most egregious forms of abuse and unfairness that I have ever encountered in my over 30 years of offering psychological therapy. The extremes of abuse they suffered included the worst forms of sexual abuse, including gang rape and rape at gunpoint. Some of the women were gunshot survivors, some had survived extreme physical abuse and domestic violence, and many had had loved ones who had committed suicide or had been murdered. All were victims of a terribly abusive environment where they had been betrayed in some fashion, by the caregivers responsible for their upbringing or by others with whom they related. From the perspective of Iconic therapy, all had developed Icons that were initially established to protect them and keep them safe. The young woman's story at the beginning of this chapter contained two powerful Icons: the abusive mother and the rapist. An overwhelming Iconic echo joined these two experiences to reverberate and repeat the mental message: "You are not worthy of life as others know it." Drawing this conclusion and thinking this way kept her safer than holding to the more dangerous view that her rights were being violated.

Most of these women, in their efforts to cope with their Iconic echoes, reflected the secret belief that they deserved the abuse ("deep down I know it was my fault"). Many suffered extreme Iconic reactions, often expressed in the form of severe addictions.

The principles of Iconic therapy were developed for the women in this program. The extreme nature of their problems led to a refinement of therapeutic strategies: if some treatment strategies did not work, they were cast aside. If an intervention did work, it was refined and improved. We discovered that deep and lasting change would occur when the Icon, that symbol of the hurt feelings, could be attacked directly. To do this, the women had to set aside their hard-wired, but counterproductive and avoidance-oriented survival strategies, and take action against the Icon. They did this not only with words but also with emotion. When they were able to do this, these women changed significantly. There was noticeable physical as well as psychological change. The light in their eyes brightened. They reported feeling lighter; that they could breathe more deeply; that they felt more confident and less angry. Self-report questionnaires confirmed their success[7]. They were on the healing journey, and they knew it. The first steps had been taken.

The same approach works for problems of lesser magnitude

When compared with the women in this program, most people's problems are minor. In general, most of us have managed to get by with these comparatively minor but still unresolved problems. Even though we manage our daily activities in spite of these historical and energized problems (stored mentally within as Icons), these Icons continually drag us down and make life harder. They corrupt us at our core with the message that we are not good enough. They diminish our self-esteem and in so doing, pollute our problem-solving efforts by discouraging healthy risk-taking. The good news is that the therapeutic strategies developed for those with extreme problems work just as powerfully on the issues of lesser magnitude that we all have to various degrees.

In Iconic language, these strategies are equally effective in addressing the Icon that represents, for example, the mildly abusive person from either your past or present. Consider, for example, the verbally abusive father whom you still love. You know that his verbal abuse was wrong, and maybe you have forgiven him, but the

---

[7] See Appendix 2 for the questionnaire results,

memory of that abuse is still painful and continues to impact your life. I have witnessed these same strategies working effectively for problems of this sort even though some might consider them minor in nature. Once you have cleared—or de-energized—these negative Icons, you are freer to focus all of your energy on the problems of the present. The strategies work effectively in both individual counselling and group therapy. I have observed their effectiveness and experienced it myself. These strategies worked for me, and I know they will work for you.

The Ultimate in Alignment

Although your survival strategies are counterproductive in the environment in which you now live, for the most part, the constellation of your efforts is perceived as normal and successful. You may not realize the almost-unconscious impact the Icon, the Iconic echo, and the Iconic reaction have upon your personality— even though these color everything within your perception. Part and parcel with your survival strategies is your effort, for safety purposes, to align yourself in some fashion with the powerful perpetrator from your past. As mentioned previously, you may strive to be agreeable and compliant in your efforts to quiet the waters and keep the peace with the abusive people in your life, especially when you are in a position of weakness. As well, when you find yourself in a position of strength with weaker ones close by, there will be moments when you become the perpetrator in your reaction to others, replicating the behavior that you detested in your own abuser. The unthinkable begins to happen: the scenario repeats. Only, this time, *you* are the abusive one. You have aligned with the perpetrator, joined his team and taken his place. You have become the perpetrator.

The Analogy That Aids Understanding

To understand the human psyche and how it functions, an analogy may be helpful. It is difficult to explain in a meaningful psychological fashion the nature of the human mind with terms such as neurons, dendrites, and axons. The developed mind organizes in terms of logic, concepts, and principles. An analogy allows these thoughts, concepts, and principles to be logically organized according to the systems contained within the analogy. When the analogy is changed, the perception of the personality is changed as well. A comparison with the therapeutic analogies used by other therapists may assist in understanding the nature of the Iconic approach.

▶ Freud's approach

Freud's theory organized the personality into three areas, each area being responsible for a unique purpose while relating internally to the others. The personality began as an entity known as the *id* (primitive urges), next the *ego* (a supervising and executive processor) grew out of the id, and then the *superego* (society's morals and directives) grew out of the ego. Freud's theory describes normal and abnormal functioning by explaining how the three components of the personality interact. Freud perceived sexual energy as the driving force for personality development. He lived in an era without birth control. There was tremendous social pressure to repress sexual interaction to avoid the complications of pregnancy. His theory often used sexual themes and presumed sexual motives for many decisions in one's life. His primary therapeutic intervention was "free association," wherein the client was encouraged to speak his or her thoughts spontaneously and thus reveal the core problems. According to Freud, insight into one's problems would lead to resolution of those problems.

▶ Cognitive behavior therapy

The more modern-day cognitive therapy is based upon the basic principle that our thoughts cause our feelings. It is a here-and-now approach, where the way a client is thinking in the present is considered the problem. Generally the client has developed an error in thinking (e.g., "I'm a bad person") and it is these erroneous thoughts that have led to problematic moods and behaviors. The therapeutic strategy involves identifying the error in thinking and then coaching the person to think more logically and realistically (e.g., "I now will practice thinking and believing that I am a good person.") It is presumed that these new and more realistic thoughts will lead to improved problem solving. This more logical thinking will engender healthy problem solving, with the attached rewards and/or positive reinforcements. Problems are not connected to the client's historical experiences but are dealt with directly. For example, if a client has developed a dependence upon alcohol in an effort to cope with physical abuse and rejection as a child, the drinking problem rather than the historical underpinnings becomes the focus. The therapeutic effort is to change the thoughts about alcohol. The underlying premise is that each problem can be solved apart from its history by challenging the unrealistic thinking. The client is cured when they have learned to think realistically so that the solutions they choose do not have at their foundation an error in thinking.

Iconic therapy

The driving force or motivating factors used in Iconic therapy is not sexually-based, as in Freud, nor is it similar to the here-and-now, error-in-thinking perspective of cognitive behavior therapy. It is *survival* based. This theory purports that **survival strategies are the foundation of every personality.**

When your survival is threatened your personality adapts to maximize the chances of surviving. Your personality is shaped, formed, and altered as it develops survival strategies based upon the traumas and life-threatening events you have endured. In fact, your personality will shape itself to minimize the risk posed by even mildly threatening events. It happens to all of us.

It is easier to understand this theory when we test it upon those who have suffered extreme trauma. As a consequence of extreme trauma, the personality structures are shaped in an equally extreme fashion to allow survival. However, the extreme shaping of the personality often leads to serious problems later. The basic approach underlying Iconic therapy is to attack the Icons within that symbolize (and energize) the past trauma. These Icons have continued to trigger survival strategies that are no longer necessary. A successful therapeutic attack on these Icons will reshape and realign the personality so that more realistic conceptions of the stressors of daily life begin to form along with more logical problem solving strategies for the problems you now face. As well, you will develop a deeper understanding and acceptance of your historical concerns.

▶ There is strong resistance to Iconic therapy

Most of those who seek out psychological treatment are initially struck with uneasiness about sharing their struggles with a stranger. Further, when it is suggested that they look deeply into the past to understand the underpinnings of their personality, the past injustices endured, and their connection to today's problems, most feel anxious and afraid. When it is suggested to clients that they should acknowledge and then defy the injustices within, they often feel quite threatened. In Iconic therapy, resistance is understood and accepted as a normal reaction to the strategies required for change.

All of us have developed strategies, or action plans, as a means to maintain a safe position in a potentially abusive or threatening environment. We have trained ourselves to minimize risks that might trigger a return of the perpetrator, a return of the unfairness, or even a return of the anxiety that was connected to the trauma we have successfully survived. Our strategies, our Iconic reactions, are so refined that we often reflexively avoid even thinking about some aspects of our abusive past. We almost automatically resist revealing the injustices we suffered, as secrecy and minimizing have been an important part of surviving. Sharing our deepest secrets has been historically perceived as a threat to survival, and this perception may remain for a lifetime. Similarly, suggestions that we change our coping strategies are reflexively judged as a threat to survival. It is almost a reflexive reaction for us to resist these suggestions. We do this because we unconsciously cling to our outdated strategies in an effort to maintain a sense of safety, security and consistency.

The resistance within

The therapeutic exercises that you will be encouraged to complete in this program go against strategies that you have instinctively developed for your survival. Your resistance to these therapeutic exercises will most likely be significant, as these exercises bring to the forefront of your consciousness the very fears you wish to avoid. In a manner similar to the clients described here, you may find it difficult to leave behind your survival behaviors that often include avoidance, denial, and minimization. You may cling to these strategies because you unconsciously adhere to the belief that to set them aside is to risk death or, from a psychological perspective, shame, humiliation, and disintegration. As well you, and possibly your therapist, may fear some form of re-traumatization if you delve too deeply into the upsetting events of the past. You cling to the way you have always been, with silence and secrecy, as this approach always seemed to work—aside from the lackluster life that remains.

For a number of reasons then, when you first witness or read about this type of therapy, your natural reaction will be to say, "No—it won't work for me!" This will be your outdated, reflexive survival strategies trying to keep you safe. It is true that these survival strategies do keep you safe, but they limit you and keep you from being all that you can be.

Walling off the threats from the past

It is presumed that your personality development was shaped, and compartmentalized, by the trauma or hard times that you managed to survive. Often with a life-threatening event, the experience is so frightening that the fear itself may incapacitate you. For those of you who survived this type of overwhelming situation, it may have been best at the time to not feel the full force of the fear, while you tried to survive. Often the fear and other strong emotions that interfered with survival are stored in a walled-off area of the personality. This serves two purposes. First, it allows for an emotion-free or emotion-reduced personality to take on the survival problems. Second, it maintains an omnipresence within that releases feeling-reminders, primarily the fear of death or humiliation, which reminds you that your survival during that previous trauma was threatened and that you need to avoid situations of a similar nature.

Thus, for survival purposes, you will find yourself continually re-experiencing aspects of the initial trauma. Often it is just the anxiety that is re-experienced. The anxiety's connection with the initial trauma or upsetting event may not be present in your consciousness. Each person, in their efforts to cope, wall off (or repress) some of the feelings and images associated with memories of abuse, abandonment and unfairness. However, even with the psychic effort required to reduce or minimize the strong emotions attached to the initial trauma ("I will just stop thinking about it") some aspect of the memory often returns, frequently triggered by reminders in the present-day environment that suggest increasing risk for further trauma or embarrassment.

Life as a child

From the very beginning, the child forms its personality in an effort to maximize chances for survival. As part of this survival strategy, all significant threats are stored as Icons to warn of impending and future danger. A survival-oriented thinking style develops that aligns the personality with the safest strategies possible in an effort to minimize threat. Later, in a non-threatening environment, this thinking style continues with the same strategies and the attached thinking errors which, at the time of the initial crisis, were functional and consistent with survival efforts.

Mental strategies for survival

As an adult, you will have moments of clarity when you realize that something is not right about your divided personality. Although you are thankful that physically you have survived injustices of the past, you come to realize that you ache for more than just that. That is why you are reading this book. Most of the time, however, you will be avoiding, sometimes unknowingly, any efforts for significant and lasting change. Every time you are visited by upsetting thoughts of the past, you will employ errors in thinking that bring about short-term relief from anxiety but leave you lost in terms of your personal development. Even when you decide that you must change your life, because the way you are living now is not working, these thoughts will bring on anxiety. When anxiety visits you, you will avoid making the difficult steps for change as your avoidance reduces your anxiety. You become lost in a self-defeating loop where anxiety triggers you to avoid the thoughts and behaviors required for change. As a consequence you remain vulnerable to initiating former self-protective, but now self-defeating, strategies that have their root connection with the Icon and are manifested as Iconic echoes within your psyche.

The Iconic Reactions

▶ The strategies that once allowed survival but now get in the way

One way of dealing with a problem that cannot be solved is to pretend that it is not a problem at all or, if it is a problem, it is an insignificant one. This is a common mental strategy that we all use in our efforts to cope. This strategy is helpful when you are not in a position to make changes—for example, when you are a child who is being verbally abused. However, when you continue to use this strategy throughout your youth, it becomes set in place within your personality. Then, of course, it becomes counterproductive in situations where your problems should be faced directly. This is an example of how an Icon (e.g., the verbally abusive mother) leads to an Iconic reaction (the silent self-condemnations) that generalizes to be included in your relationships as an adult.

This same principle applies to the therapeutic situation. When you attend a therapist, wanting to change, it will be natural for you to continue to practice the ingrained coping strategies that allowed you to get to this point in your life. Unfortunately these same strategies will make it very difficult for the therapist to comprehend the nature of the problem that even you, because you have been denying its existence, may not understand. Below are the Iconic reactions that form when you try to minimize, rationalize or deny the nature of your problems.

Minimizing

Your first strategy in getting control of unsettling thoughts brought on by your trauma is to pretend that the trauma and its aftermath were not as bad as initially perceived. You will try to trick yourself into minimizing the negative impact of what happened to you. The

Iconic reaction may be: "The … [abusive or traumatic experience] was not that bad."

Rationalizing

You will rationalize the experience, trying to find good reasons for having endured what occurred: "I really learned from that. It was kind of a good thing. It made me tougher. Anyway, I probably deserved it."

Denying

One of the most irrational errors in thinking is denial. You will begin to deny any trauma or negative experience occurred: "I'll pretend it didn't happen, and if I pretend hard enough, it will disappear from my memory."

Blaming

This is an overarching error in thinking that is very common. When a problem is presented, there is a tendency, caused by inadequacy, to avoid the problem by blaming others or a higher power for causing the problem. The over-arching blaming scenario begins as follows:

> I blame the trauma for destroying my life. When things continually go badly, I will presume there is a curse that God or some other powerful force has placed on me. This is the cause of my unhappiness. I will accept the conclusion that my life is cursed, that nothing will work out. This will give me permission to not try anymore or not try as hard as I should. When I am really low, I will just give up. I will just go through the motions. I will be helpless. It's not my fault! I blame fate itself for a life where I manage only a minimal existence and an unhappy one at that.

Often blaming strategies spread to problems of daily life where blaming others for a current problem is erroneously presumed to be a solution rather than choosing efforts that deal more directly with the problem:

If you hadn't aggravated me, I won't have got so upset.
It's all your fault.
If you had only reminded me that I had an appointment,
I would have been there.

While these strategies may offer some comfort and a temporary reduction in anxiety, they do not eliminate the source of the negative energy within, the Icon. This negative energy is triggered into consciousness at a frequency and intensity that your coping strategies prevent you from realizing. These coping strategies—these errors in thinking—allow for the continued existence of the Icon and all of the negative self-loathing thoughts and unproductive thinking errors that emanate. Even with the implementation of strategies to take the focus of your thoughts away from long-past negative events, the entity that deals with threats to survival, the Icon, remains submerged in the unconscious but close enough to the surface to easily trigger ominous warnings that negative, possibly overwhelming events are about to occur. This keeps you continually on edge.

▶ Robbed of potential

The Icon, the energized memory of the abuser or the abusive situation, continues to live within you. It has an energy and life force of its own. The Icon has a constant symbolic and mental presence and serves as an ongoing reminder. The Icon continues to emit visual and feeling memories of past traumatic events when triggered by environmental cues that remind you of what occurred. Sometimes the denial strategy is so strong that the memory of the frightening situation is repressed ("I don't know why I am so worried and jumpy all the time"), but the signals from the forgotten, yet omnipresent, Icon continue in the form of anxiety and apprehension. The presence of the Icon within robs you of your potential for growth and the actualization of your true self. It holds you to the past: to the trauma, the suffering, and the self-condemnation connected to your coping strategies.

Life as an adult

Negative Icons live within all of us who have not achieved our true potential. For those who have suffered terribly abusive beginnings, the Icons are powerful and often out of control in their efforts to protect you at any cost (including the cost of future growth). Those of you who have found high levels of maturity have faced your Icons and overcome them. For those of you who still struggle, and you are in the majority, a series of therapeutic strategies has been developed to allow you to find relief from the haunting repetitions of your Ionic echo and your personalized Iconic reaction—the voices within that limit you. These are the voices that tell you not to venture forth to take on many of the challenges of everyday life, because they are perceived as too dangerous. These are the voices that remind you to be careful, to be extra cautious, because hurtfulness may be waiting, as it was before. It is these forces that remind you (through your errors in thinking) that you not only deserved the abuse of yesterday but also that it might happen again, because you still deserve it. These are the forces that keep you anxious most of the time, especially during those times when you consider making changes in the way you are living. These forces tell you that it is best to stick with what you know, your cautious strategies.

Let me remind you and encourage you. No one has to carry inner messages reminding them that they are not worthy of a full life in which they can actualize all of their potentialities. No one has to live forever with the fears and the condemnations of yesterday.

CHAPTER 4
What Is Really Happening?

I was asked to write down what I would say to you [the man who sexually abused me for a year when I was eleven] if I ever encountered you, or what I would just like to say to you. I find this hard. I haven't thought about this on purpose, ever.

...It is easier for me not to think about you, or what you did to me or what I feel. It amazes me how your actions, done so many years ago, still control my thoughts. I cannot freely think or feel what I want, and that is wrong. ...

You broke me emotionally and mentally! I am a broken person because of you. I should be yelling, screaming and breaking everything in sight—and in those moments when I do have these feeling I push them down and refuse them. I won't allow myself to act on them, out of fear that I may lose control. That's all my life it seems was about—control.

I had finally put you behind me, or so I thought, but I was just deluding myself. In fact, I took it out on those that I loved the most. My family had to endure my volatility and rage, mostly fueled I feel by you. … My kids did not get the father they should have … I hate blame—it's an excuse … but you created my monster within … I was too weak to face this as a child, too scared to face my demons as a child, it was easier for me to bury it all, pretend. Look where that got me! … I hate you more than is ever possible. … I hate that you still have that power over me. You don't deserve to occupy even a since cell of my brain—but smack there you are. Everything comes back to you and I hate myself for this.

Many of you have had destructive and devastating experiences in youth and later in life that limit your personal growth. It is these events, and your efforts to survive them, that later interfere with your ability to achieve your potential.

At this stage in the explanation of Iconic therapy, let us focus on some of the primary scenarios of abuse. Once a person has been mistreated, memories of the experience establish and maintain a presence within the mind, and as long as it lives there, this presence inhibits personal growth. There are two primary areas of mistreatment that cause many people to suffer from psychological problems. The first is mistreatment by parents, which would include abandonment, neglect, verbal abuse, and physical abuse. The second is any form of assault, whether it be sexual, physical, or verbal. These types of events, even after they have ended, often continue to haunt the developing personality. They are the root cause of many psychological problems, including ongoing feelings of depression, anxiety, and self-condemnation. Other sources of trauma that lead to psychological issues will be introduced later.

If you are one of those individuals who have endured these types of events, you are a survivor of the highest order. You have shaped your personality by developing uniquely designed, well-ingrained strategies to survive the very difficult problems that were forced upon you early in your life. While these strategies are no longer necessary, your instinct to continue to use them persists. You survived, but now you pay a terrible price, as your journey beyond mere survival is very much compromised. Generally, for those of you who suffered extreme levels of abuse, you have had to adopt self-soothing addictive strategies offered by the community around you. Generally, the first offering was food; the second, alcohol; the third, medication; the fourth, illicit drugs and then a multitude of choices for comfort from other forms of addiction. Any self-soothing behavior will serve to distract you from that never-ending Iconic echo ("You're not good enough to achieve at high levels") and the personalizing of that concept ("I'm just not worthy"). Self-soothing behaviors offer you comfort but also become an addiction. They serve to soften your deeply rooted reflex for self-condemnation, which years ago aligned you with the mindset of the perpetrator of your abuse and kept you safer. Only if you are very desperate will you attend a psychologist, and when there, you will report—*your self-diagnosis*—that you suffer from addiction, anxiety, and possibly anger and frustration for your current situation. It is most likely that your core problems, *the abuse and injustice you endured*, will at first not be mentioned.

We are all survivors of past abuse, mistreatment, and injustice. In the present, some of you will look back and trick yourself into thinking, "I made it through that mess. I'm glad it's over." However, for most of you, it is not over. Ingrained strategies and philosophies designed for an earlier time period of life remain; these allowed survival but now get in the way. From my perspective, to all of you I say:

Congratulations. You survived the problems of your developmental years. You are now submersed in adulthood with all of its freedoms and responsibilities. You made it! Unfortunately, the survival strategies that worked so well to get you this far are no longer helpful or beneficial. In fact, these strategies, honed to perfection during your early years, are now counterproductive and may lead to your destruction or extremely limit your personal development.

How Did This All Happen?

How did we get to this place where we are all tangled up, some of us much more than others? How did we become persons seeking safety, sanctuary, and separation more than healthy risk-taking, commitment, and connection? Why is it that we carry frustration, anger, and discouragement within rather than acceptance, peacefulness, and optimism? What is the context of our society, community, and family that have served as precursors to the misery of so many?

The Basic Concepts

What follows are the basic concepts that evolved as this theory was developing. These concepts will explain the nature of your current development and the way your journey is similar to that of others. You are not alone, although you may think you are. The principles are the same for all of us. We are all impacted by the same survival forces that initially saved us but now limit us. It is just that some of you suffered more extreme abuse and, as a consequence, had to develop more extreme solutions.

▶ Concept 1: The flawed environment engenders survival strategies to cope with trauma

The conditions for growth and development are rarely ideal

The nature of the human condition is fraught with problems. Often we come from a place that was not perfectly structured. To find maturity, we must realize the impact of the conditions under which we evolved. We need to come to know and understand, for example, that all parents and caregivers, including our own, are human. Some parents were badly abused, and their ability to parent was therefore damaged. Parents often pass on abuse to their children. We do not condemn our parents. We only want to understand them and their impact on us, their children.

Flawed child-rearing practices

Many parents base their child-rearing practices on the way they were raised. Their models for parenting were encouraged and shaped not only by the flawed parents who preceded them but also by the less-than-fair mores and dictates of the society in which they lived. The society of one generation is often very much out of synch and incompatible with the next. Confusion regarding child rearing is often generated from this incompatibility. Yet, we know that the basic needs for children and their development remain constant across generations. All children need to be loved and nurtured by caring and concerned parents. They need their parents to have a loving presence in their lives and to serve as role models for the basic nature of human relating—to demonstrate respect for the rights of others while at the same time defending and establishing healthy personal boundaries. Children need a nurturing parent-child relationship to find and consolidate their individuality and integrity.

The flawed parents and caregivers

I believe that many problems begin when basic child-rearing principles are violated. Parents, parental substitutes, and care-givers make mistakes, often unknowingly, that can hurt or traumatize the developing child. The child survives, grows, and copes with the flawed parents and flawed environment by developing strategies that address, but seldom resolve, the problems presented.

It happens to many of us

It is in the nature of the human condition for one generation to repeat the flawed child rearing, abusive conduct, and possibly trauma-inducing experiences to which they were exposed, often (but not always) in a milder form. As a consequence, most human beings suffer some harmful child-rearing events. Many who suffered terrible abuse as children, in their desperation to defend their fragile nature, break out of the restrictions of their youth by modelling the abusive nature of their caregivers. This may lead them to violate the rights of others. In extreme cases criminal solutions may be chosen. If you were lucky, the abusive events you endured were relatively mild or—if your abuse was extreme—there were less damaging (non-criminal) solutions available for you.

It is possible to recover from the abusive experiences of the past with the therapeutic strategies I have developed. I have worked with many individuals who have recovered to find a life of promise and potential.

▶ Concept 2: Silence and secrecy are the first strategies for survival

Based on the premise "children are to be seen but not heard," parents often mistakenly condemn their children for "backtalk" when, as adults, they will be expected to offer an opinion or engage in a debate. In some situations, especially those of an abusive nature, it is often better, in terms of survival perceptions, for children to be silent rather than to speak their thoughts. As a child's verbal skills are in the early stages of development, and as silence is, in abusive relationships, often encouraged over valid protest, it is natural for a child to choose silence as a means of coping with the stressors brought on by abuse.

In general then, the most frequently used strategy for the mildly, moderately, and severely abused child is silence and its extension, secrecy. With silence and secrecy, there is a sense of safety and a thinking style as follows:

> I won't protest the wrongness of the abuse and its unfairness. If I do, it could get worse, and I could be hurt more. If I just keep silent and don't attract attention, maybe not getting noticed will mean it won't happen again. At least it is not happening now, and I can be thankful for that.

For the child being sexually, physically, or verbally abused, silence and secrecy may serve a purpose beyond survival, that of protecting others. For example, sometimes the child is making a noble effort to sacrifice themselves for the sake of others. They may come to the following conclusions:

> I have to keep what my stepdad is doing a secret because if I tell, the only family I have and the only family my siblings have, will be destroyed. I need my family to survive.

When children come to believe that secrecy and silence are the best strategies available to survive the abusive events and to protect those they love; their ability to express themselves in social situations as adults is often damaged. Unfortunately, the damage that results has two dimensions. First, and most obvious, adults who inherited these survival strategies from youth struggle in most situations that require spontaneous communication. They may find it difficult to express their honest opinions. This difficulty with communication may hamper their development in a number of ways. Second, as they so often practiced silence for safety purposes during youth, a change to spontaneity feels unnatural and is judged unconsciously or intuitively as a risk to survival or security. It follows that they will be prone to carry these habits of silence and secrecy forward into adulthood and, out of habit, use them when reacting during stressful events and in general, when facing life's difficult problems.

▶ Concept 3: Alignment with the abuser is a natural means of survival

Certain thinking strategies are essential for survival when an individual is being victimized and mistreated, especially when the abuse continues over a period of time. When experiencing mild and even extreme forms of abuse over time, it is often necessary to develop a mindset that is consistent with the abusing person. For example, it may be best to think along these lines:

> My best chance for survival is to keep this abusive person happy; therefore, I will seek out his perspective. I will, if not accept; at least consider his philosophy of life. In accordance with that philosophy, it is okay for me to be abused in certain situations. From his perspective [the abuser's], I deserved it because maybe I was bad that one time. It's okay to let it keep happening, because I am too weak to stop it. Besides, letting it happen and going along with it will keep me alive. If I protest, it could be worse.

As well, it is very common for a victim of abuse to admit that she or he would sacrifice herself/himself so that a sibling will not be abused.

> I will let him abuse me, and then he won't want to abuse my younger sister. I will let him think that it is okay to hurt me (alignment) in my effort to protect my sister and my mother.

Sexual abuse is one extreme example of childhood mistreatment that often triggers these survival efforts. However, physical abuse, verbal abuse, and abandonment concerns may lead to the same thought processes.

What begins as a few moments of complicity, silence, and secrecy to keep the abuser happy over the time period of abuse may extend afterwards for a month, or a year, or ten years. For many, in your aligning attitudes and conduct, you may come to accept (partially or wholly) the abuser's assertion that you are of less value than others. You come to the belief that in some fashion you deserved the abuse and you may hold to this view for a lifetime. Furthermore, your vulnerability to finding yourself in another abusive situation is reinforced by your thoughts and actions that support a similar form of compliance with a new abuser and a resignation to a fate that you have always known. As well, your easily retrieved fears of abuse find a permanent place in your personality and leave you in a constant state of mild (or stronger) anxiety, sometimes with and sometimes without a clear memory of the initial abuse.

Even when the abuse has stopped you, the victim, continue to remain aligned with the abuser through your silence and secrecy— gathering your breath and being thankful you are alive, that your secrets are safe, and that nobody knows. However, you remain always watchful in case the abuser, or the abusive situation or a sign or predictor of abuse, will return. You pray that it will never happen again and that your horrible secret will never be revealed. You always remember that if you continue the secrecy the abuser will not be upset with you.

It is like being at war and having found a safe foxhole (of silence) to hide in while the bullets fly over you. You cherish your safety in the little place that you have found. The memories of the abuse and the fear of the perpetrator continue to hold you in that one safe place. It becomes an unspoken contract: "Keep the secret, keep the silence, and the evil won't return." This extends to "Keep the secret until the memory fades, until it feels as if it never really happened. If it never really happened, then no one ever needs to know."

Secrecy and silence are often adopted as the best survival strategies to align with the abuser. This problem-solving approach encourages and supports a distorted thinking style that is effective for survival but counterproductive and damaging when used to address the problems of everyday life that lie ahead. As you move forward in your journey, this strategy of alignment leaves you stressed, and anxious that somehow others will find out something about you that you hoped would never be revealed.

▶ Concept 4: Shame is a natural consequence of aligning with the injustices suffered

One complication with alignment and secrecy is shame. The feelings of shame have three dimensions. First, there is the shame of complicit involvement. The accompanying thought may be as follows:

> I was involved in something shameful. It happened in my family, with someone I trusted. In some way, it must have been my fault or at least partially my fault. I must have done something to deserve what happened. I am ashamed.

Second, there is shame for one's inaction. The accompanying thought may be something like this:

> A bad thing happened to me. I should have done something about it. I am ashamed that I didn't do anything. Now others will think that I thought it was okay. I should have protested. I should have told someone. Now it's too late. Now I've just got to get over it. I am ashamed that it still bothers me. I am ashamed that I just can't forget it. I now feel ashamed that I can't stop thinking about it.

Third, there is the shame for not expressing your longing to release deep feelings of anger, hatred, and disgust for what happened. The shame emanates from continuing to suppress your true self, when you know that you have a voice that longs to speak the truth. The accompanying thoughts are a jumble of feelings, often of anger, for the abuser and for oneself:

For the abuser: I hate that bastard for doing that. If I could, I would kill him. I would have justice. I have to have revenge.

For the self: I hate myself for being part of that. Sometimes I wish I could just die so I won't have to live with the memory of it. It must have been my fault. I'm pissed off for not telling, because he's doing it to someone else. Now that's my fault. I'm a despicable person. I hate myself for being a coward. I should have done something to stop it.

The longer you hold the secret, the greater the shame for feeling you were somehow responsible (complicit involvement), that you should have taken action to defend yourself and others (inaction), and that somehow you no longer should be harboring deep, unexpressed feelings of anger and hatred for both the abuser and yourself.

Shame is the primary mechanism that keeps you from attending therapy and from trying to resolve the problem by going outside of yourself to speak to someone else. I say the following to encourage and support you:

Break free of the shame that holds you back and keeps you so confined. Go to a therapist, or counsellor, or a trusted, wise friend. Share with them what happened. Counsellors have heard stories similar to yours many times. They will listen and understand. They will not be shocked. You will find great comfort in finally sharing the truth you always suspected and now will have confirmed: namely, that the shame was never yours. It belongs to that person who treated you so unfairly.

Silence, secrecy, alignment, and the shame that follows continue to have a mental presence for an extended period of time, perhaps for the rest of your life. That is because these components were, and continue to be, the foundation for your survival strategies, albeit a meagre type of survival, where only the bare minimum in life can be accessed. (It is not much fun in a foxhole.) But life goes on in the meantime.

You become a divided person. On the exterior, you present as perfectly normal, as if the abuse never occurred. The interior is the opposite. You hold yourself at the ready, prepared for the return of the abuser, or the abusive situation, or someone who reminds you of the abuser. You were initially terrified and, over time, the feelings of terror subsided but you remained continually apprehensive. You fear not only the return of abuse but also the exposure of your true and very vulnerable, almost defenseless self. You fear that the secret shame you carry will inadvertently be discovered. If the truth becomes known, then you fear that you will be humiliated and ridiculed. As well, you fear that your long-lasting sense of anger and hatred—not only for the abuser but also for your own sense of inadequacy—will be released. You worry that this type of emotional release will be very uncomfortable, upsetting and embarrassing. If this emotional release does occur, you fear that it will fail to bring the justice you deserve and further, you fear it may bring more misery.

In general, shame is the most primitive and powerful Iconic reaction. The shame holds you to silence and initially supported survival, but with the continuation of the shaming process, your efforts to leave the past and to find resolution and release are blocked. You strive to be normal, but you are filled with a secret shame that will not leave you. You long to find and release your true self but, from years of practice, you keep quiet when your voice should be heard. You are no longer able to speak with a sincere voice, as your words are shrouded with fear and anxiety. You feel a disconnection from your own feelings which you have trained yourself to suppress. In your efforts to survive, you have lost your essence.

▶ Concept 5: Errors in thinking form to hide and justify the cesspool of shame and secrecy

Even though there are errors in thinking regarding how you process and conceptualize the trauma or negative experience you endured (the way you understand your problems), there is also a constellation of errors in thinking regarding how you conceptualize the nature of your personhood as well (the way you understand yourself). It is natural to personalize the initial abusive message from the Icon. For example, the error in thinking—"I'm a worthless person"—may initially support the survival of childhood abuse. This thinking style has a protective purpose, as it aligns you with the abuser and may keep you safer. However, this Iconic reaction is counterproductive to later personal growth.

When you think about it, to classify this coping strategy (aligning with/pleasing the abuser) as an error in thinking is a misnomer. As pointed out above, this alignment is a survival tactic that involves personal sacrifice to protect oneself and possibly others in the family. Unfortunately and tragically, these initial efforts also lead to the loss of personal integrity and are the first steps towards self-condemnation. A strategy that may have had its foundation in personal survival and, as well, concern for others ("I'll keep quiet to protect the family") evolves to one of self-denigration ("I'll keep quiet because I don't deserve to be heard"). When used out of habit, in non-threatening conditions, this strategy eventually evokes errors in thinking that are long lasting and counterproductive to personal growth.

> I've been abused by the people I needed and trusted the most. They said I deserved it, and I guess they are right. I suppose if I want to abuse myself with food,

alcohol, drugs, or sex, well, that's okay. There's some comfort in that. If I want to give myself sexually to some stranger for a warm moment or for money, that's a lot better than what was happening to me. At least I feel like I have a little bit of control.

Iconic therapy will help you in your efforts to identify these thought distortions and shut down this destructive thinking and very limiting Iconic reaction. Below are a number of thinking errors listed with their connection to a troubling or traumatic event.

Trauma/Injustice Experienced	Iconic Reaction *(Thinking errors and distorted thoughts that may develop)*
Abandonment by parents	Deep down there is something wrong with me that makes me unlovable; that's why my parents never loved me; that's why I ended up in foster care. *(Thinking error: "I'm ashamed to admit I'm unlovable. I am ashamed. I am unlovable.")*
Sexual abuse as a child	The world is an unsafe place. I can't trust anyone. It's okay to sacrifice myself for the abuser. If I don't, I may die or my family may be destroyed. It is best to think they are more worthy than me. I am less worthy, at times worthless. It is better to keep quiet and let them have the limelight. The rights of my family, my parents, and my siblings are more important than my rights. *(Thinking error: "I'm worthless.")*

Physical abuse	I deserve to be punched when I'm bad. It is mainly because I am a bad person, not worthy of the affection of others. I should hate my abuser for hitting me, but it is wiser to adopt his philosophy; I will hate myself. *(Thinking error: "I'm a despicable person.")*
Verbal abuse ("You're stupid")	I'm little and not smart enough to counter that accusation. I'll just stop trying. Challenging the ones in power will lead to more personal humiliation. It is in my best interest, at this point, to agree with them: I'm not that smart. It's pointless for me to try at school or university, because I don't have the brain power. My father/ mother/teacher was right—I can't do this homework, and it's useless to try. *(Thinking error: "I'm not intelligent.")*
Wartime trauma	My body feels that the war has not ended. That person that looks normal is carrying a gun, or maybe it is that person behind me. I have to remain on guard, or I will die. *(Thinking error: "I'm always in danger.")*

If you are carrying any of these errors in thinking understand that they are interfering with your ability to face the issues of everyday life. As well, know that these errors in thinking are not true. You are a worthy person. You only began to think otherwise as a means of surviving. In the present, you do not need to be inundated with these self-defeating thoughts every time a stressful challenge presents itself. These thoughts no longer serve any useful purpose. They need to be eliminated from your mindset, and they *can* be with the use of the therapeutic exercises that will be discussed later.

▶ Concept 6: Resentment, anger, and hatred begin to form as a consequence of injustices suffered in silence

Errors in thinking, built upon compliance with the injustice of the perpetrator and the shame attached, after reverberating for years will cause feelings of resentment, anger, and hatred. These feelings when actualized may lead to the harming of others, which is the ultimate alignment with the abuser. When you harbour these long-standing resentments, it becomes easy to justify your own abusive behavior with another layer of erroneous thinking:

> In some situations it is okay to abuse others—not sexually, but verbally it is okay, and physically, if you have to. Let's face it, the abuse I dish out is not half as bad as what I got. It's only fair—I suffered so much—they deserve to suffer too. If I have to steal from someone else—well, they're not my people, not my family; they never had it as bad as me—a little loss won't hurt them much.

For the child living with the alcoholic father, the strategies are similar and often have a noble beginning: to protect the reputation of the family:

> It's best to keep Dad's drinking problem a secret—I want all the other kids to think we have a great family, even if we don't.

Later the error in thinking shifts:

> Men have special privileges in the family. They work
> hard, and when they're tired, they are allowed to get
> drunk and say what they want; that's what being a man
> is all about.

It is not a giant leap to become the abuser and continue the
cycle of abuse:

> I am a man, and as a man, if I want, I can get drunk,
> and then my wife just better listen to me—the kids, too.

The first strategy for survival is alignment and compliance,
as previously noted. Generally, as a victim of abuse, you are in
the weaker position and may not have the physical prowess or the
verbal skills to defend your boundaries and integrity. Thus, you
comply with the abuse forced upon you. Internally, however, you
begin to resent the violations of dignity that you have been forced
to endure. As you mature, in those moments between the abusive
events or even long after the abuse has stopped, you begin to realize
and comprehend the magnitude of the injustices you have suffered.

Over time, your resentment builds to anger and, in its extreme
form, hatred. These feelings spill over into other areas of your life.
For those of you with an extreme history of abuse, you may find that
your anger is released in situations where it is out of proportion to the
unfairness you experience in the present. You yelled at your boss, or
you can't forgive your partner; you bullied your child and justified
it, or you were rougher in your sporting endeavours than you should
have been. You may have developed temper-control problems. When
you think about attending counselling, you are afraid that your
anger may get the best of you or that its excesses will be revealed,
even when only discussing the past abusive events.

There are many men in prison who have intervened when their fathers assaulted their mothers. As boys they were beaten by their fathers. Then, when they gained the physical strength to challenge their fathers, they turned the tables and beat them physically. These men often have at their core a deep well of resentment that is easily triggered into violence, a violence that leads to convictions for assault.

Many of you who have endured physical abuse from parenting figures, even those of you who only suffered verbal abuse, have developed a general distrust in relating to others, especially those in positions of authority. This is the approach that has allowed those of you exposed to physical violence and verbal abuse in youth to survive the indignities forced upon you.

If you are one of the unfortunate ones raised with violence as a key component in your relationship with your father or mother, most likely you will have the propensity to become extremely angry when upset. You may find that when discussing with your counsellor your relationship with your angry father for example, you become quite angry. When working with you on these deep and troubling issues, your psychologist or counsellor will need to continually monitor and review the nature of your feelings, especially when you are becoming emotional. Your therapist will remind you that you need to control your feelings of anger even when you are speaking about those same feelings.

> How are you doing right now? I can see that you are becoming angry. Is your anger for me? If you feel you will lose control, you are allowed to leave. It is important to remember that to speak about your anger without being overwhelmed is the first step. It is important that you are able to deal with your anger without hitting anyone. Remember, I am on your side, and together we are working on your problem with anger.

All of us have to remember that it is very important, as part of our healing journey, to be able to express our emotions in a controlled fashion, especially our feelings of anger and disappointment. If you are a person who, when stressed, begins to yell and scream and to consider striking others, you should first acknowledge that this type of reaction is a problem for you and needs to be addressed.

Please understand that you have become abusive and disrespectful towards others in your efforts to cope with the abuse and disrespect you endured. It is a manifestation of the Icon within, the abusive authority figure that lives within you. This is the authority figure you aligned with for survival purposes. To survive you had to suppress your feelings of anger for that person. As part of your Iconic reaction you are now, quite possibly, using similarly aggressive behaviors and attitudes to release anger, resentment and even hatred aggressively, inappropriately and unfairly on to others in your life who should not have to endure toxic emotions meant for someone else.

▶ Concept 7: Personal survival is not our only need

One's personal survival is the most primitive need and serves as the foundation for human motivation. However, it is not our only need. Once our basic survival objectives have been met, other needs surface, needs connected to the continuance and enhancement of the human species. Once the abuse has stopped basic survival problems are no longer a pressing concern. Nevertheless, even though the abuse or injustice no longer occurs, you still cannot leave your deeply ingrained survival tactics. As a result, you will fail, or at least suffer more than you have to, in your efforts to achieve the fulfillment of the higher-order, survival of the species, needs. You may struggle to find and express love, closeness, and intimacy. It will be difficult for you to trust enough for intimacy, or you may trust too much. When you do manage to establish a relationship, your relating style may be filled with errors in thinking as described above. If you are a victim of sexual or physical abuse, you may experience shame and confusing thoughts that interfere with intimacy:

> Will my partner be able to tell that, deep down, I believe I am unlovable? Will he come to know that because I have always been unlovable, it was somehow okay that I was mistreated? If he finds out, will he think it was somehow my fault? Will he ever forgive me for being such a loser? Will he understand when I tell him I did other things that I am ashamed of that were somehow connected? I can't trust him enough to share that. I am not really worthy of his love. I will keep the mistreatment a secret. I hope it doesn't drive a wedge between us. [If you were sexually abused the following thoughts may also occur.] I feel that sex is so disgusting; I can't manage it as an expression of loving. Every time I have sex with my partner, I think of that time when …

Therefore, our personal survival is not our only need. We long to contribute to the next generation by connecting with a loved one; by having children; by working towards creating a family, a community, a nation, a world where others are safe and respected and children are nurtured. We want to actualize these natural desires for an improved human condition with passion and conviction. We long for meaningful work and a purpose for our existence. But our longing is thwarted by the Icons within that hold us to our primitive need to survive the abuse of the past and to repeat the errors in thinking we put in place to aid that survival.

► Concept 8: We are all afflicted with negative Iconic echoes that interfere with how we contemplate and then initiate future action

No one escapes the negative propaganda generated by the destructive Iconic echo within ("You're not good enough"). As human beings, we are flawed, and we are raised by people with flaws. We live in a culture that is filled with injustice, especially injustice for the vulnerable: children, minorities, and seniors. Children are easy targets for adults damaged by their own unresolved history of trauma. Your parents and mine inherited child-rearing strategies that are now known to be damaging. We have all developed negative Icons within that remind us of the injustices we endured and threaten us with their continuance.

To find your true self, to take on that journey to maturity and integrity, you must find a means of overcoming the abuse you suffered as a child, teenager, and young adult. The problematic Iconic echoes that formed initially enhanced our survival and are inculcated within all of us, some more than others. This, I believe, is an unrecognized constant in the human condition. To a certain extent, we are all like the prisoners I treated. We all have been abused in some fashion, and we continue to actualize our survival strategies to avoid further abuse. We continue to be visited by Iconic themes and messages that compromise and limit our sense of self.

Fortunately, for most of us, the abuse was not as extreme as that endured by the prisoners with whom I worked; but to the extent that abuse was present for each of us, it has had its impact. As a victim of abuse, deceit, or injustice, you inevitably developed your own Iconic echo and the errors in thinking that follow. In the past these helped you cope, but now they interfere with the potential you can and should achieve.

▶ Concept 9: We all develop Iconic reactions— counterproductive thoughts and behaviors that soften the pain of past injustice but interfere with our potential to achieve

We are all vulnerable to developing thoughts and behaviors consistent with the Iconic echoes ("You're not good enough") we heard as children. We personalize these voices to make them our own ("I'm not good enough"). Once we practice these self-condemning thoughts over numerous repetitions we are prone to give up when extra effort is required for success. As well, we are more vulnerable turn to addictions to soften the accompanying anxiety that is generated by our self-condemnations. Addictions, especially those supported by the media and our heritage, are common Iconic reactions. Excessive indulgence in food, alcohol, medication, and illicit drugs distract us from a constant sense of anxiety and mitigate the painful and repetitious reminders of past hurts. These indulgences become powerful coping mechanisms that soften the Iconic reactions that we know at one level are not true, but at another, feeling level, believe and feel deeply. Sometimes the source of these Iconic themes is forgotten or hidden in the unconscious. The addiction remedies chosen momentarily take away painful memories and constant self-doubting, but they interfere with our longing for personal fulfillment.

When your longing for integrity, love, and accomplishment is frustrated by the self-condemning messages that aligned you with the perpetrators of past injustices, you are left to live a desperate life, filled with anxiety, frustration, resentment, anger, and ongoing (but secret) self-loathing. Most of you will manage to arrange a moderately satisfying life, even with problem-solving strategies that have been compromised by errors in thinking. Your pleasure-seeking activities will be supported by mild to moderate addictions. You will find enough satisfaction through small successes at work and mild intoxication every weekend to get by. You will not attend a psychologist or counsellor, as your need to change is not stronger than the secrecy, shame, and guilt you carry for the unjustified abuse you suffered. As well, your willingness to accept less than what could be is primarily an expression of your secret fear of being discovered as less worthy than you truly are. You hold this ongoing apprehension that others will learn that you are really not good enough to have even what you have legitimately achieved. This fear binds you to the mediocre lifestyle for which you have settled.

You are left on the inside of yourself looking out, longing for more—the nature of which you often erroneously translate into a longing for material possessions and escape. ("If I could only have a Lexus, or that trip to Hawaii, I would be happy. I would be the person I want to be.")

I am always saddened by the human potential that is lost in the sacrifices people make to hold onto crippling errors in thinking. To live with and endure Iconic echoes that continually remind you of your worthlessness is a very tragic state of existence.

I recommend that all of you take the steps I write about below. You will find that your errors in thinking will fade; the Iconic message that you are not good enough will stop; and, finally, your unresolved anger and resentment will leave you.

► A diagram for clarity

What follows are illustrations that explain how the personality is formed. The personality is conceptualize as an elliptical form. As shown in Phase I, in the bottom ellipse, the dynamic quality of the personality is seen as survival energy that is central to its functioning. This survival energy is channeled through the True Self, the essence of one's personality. This energy pushes the essence of the person (the True Self) forward in time, place and in a direction that enhances survival (for the self, for the species). This energy is expressed, in the early stages of life by primarily maintaining and insuring an individual's safety and, from a cognitive perspective, their integrity. In a nurturing environment the person is open to the stimuli presented but remains vulnerable as well.

The person generally meets with adversity in their journey forward. Most adversity is mild and addressed easily with slight changes in direction, behavior and cognition. However, some adversity is life-threatening and results in major changes not only for direction, behavior and cognition but also in the structure of the personality itself. An Icon forms, as shown in the upper ellipse, as an early warning indicator that a threatening event, previously experienced, may re-occur.

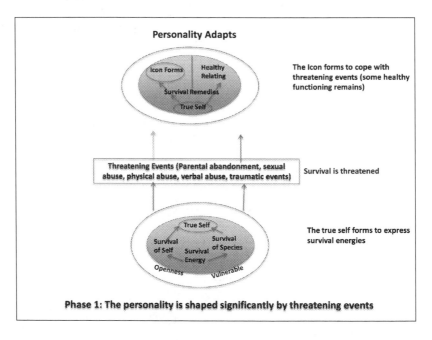

Personality Adapts

Icon Forms | Healthy Relating

Survival Remedies

True Self

The Icon forms to cope with threatening events (some healthy functioning remains)

Threatening Events (Parental abandonment, sexual abuse, physical abuse, verbal abuse, traumatic events)

Survival is threatened

True Self

Survival of Self | Survival of Species

Survival Energy

Openness | Vulnerable

The true self forms to express survival energies

Phase 1: The personality is shaped significantly by threatening events

Phase 2 shows, in the bottom ellipse, how the Icon is expressed through the Iconic Echo (inner warning messages) and the Iconic Reaction (reactive cognitive interpretations and safety oriented behaviors). These two components, although functional during the initial traumatic event, later trigger errors in thinking and confused problem-solving strategies in desperate efforts to find safety and security, especially when reacting to environmental reminders of the initial trauma. Unfortunately these confused efforts lead primarily to feelings of frustration, anger, shame and guilt. Addiction behaviors often follow as a means relieving inner feelings of fear and anxiety. Finally, there are some aspects of everyday life that are not affected by the trauma experience and for these, realistic thinking and healthy relating follow.

In the center of the Phase 2 diagram is a rectangle representing the application of the seven steps involved in the Iconic Therapy program which in order are: 1. Disclosure, 2. Role Play, 3. Cloak of Shame, 4. Advocacy, 5. Speech to the Community, 6. Breaking Free and 7. My Journey so Far. After the therapeutic exercises have been completed the personality, in its healed form, emerges as shown in the upper ellipse. The person (the True Self) is now able to apply logical problem solving strategies to the problems of daily living without the interference of the Iconic Echoes and Iconic Reactions. They are now more able to love and commit. They begin to develop an interest in the well-being of others. Urges to indulge in addictive behaviors are reduced and environmental stimuli that remind the person of the previous traumatic experiences are no longer so easily triggered into consciousness.

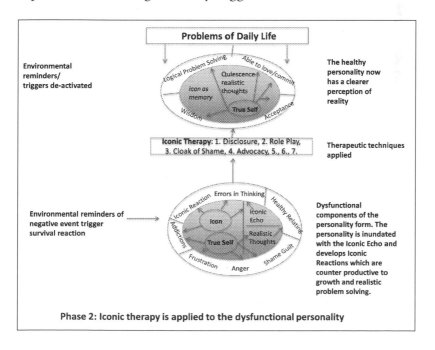

Phase 2: Iconic therapy is applied to the dysfunctional personality

CHAPTER 5
The Problem, The Solution, The Resistance

I honestly would rather forget the past—pretend that it never happened—but it is part of me. It made me who I am today. The abuse from my mother; being sexually, mentally, and physically abused by my ex; being raped at the age of 13—all have had a huge impact on the person I am today. I have an eating disorder, addiction problems, I used to and still sometimes do hit myself when I have feelings that I don't want to feel—because every time I did feel something, it was numbed out of me by fists. I know now that it is okay to talk and to feel, to not have to be or feel ashamed of the past, to forgive when you are ready. That it is okay to be yourself. I am still learning to be okay with everything, but what I know is that there are women out there just like me and you, and that together we are stronger, that it is okay to talk about what happened to you. I am still changing. The biggest one is standing up for myself and believing that I am worth it. And I know and want to share that no matter what the feelings, it's worth talking about it!

The Problem

▶ Part 1: Early survival strategies cause problems later

Each generation, in their efforts to raise the next generation—to mentor and guide, to nurture and love—makes mistakes. Our forbearers carried with them errors in thinking and confused efforts to find personal justice at the expense of children and vulnerable others around them. Their acts of unfairness caused problems we must now face. These abusive acts planted a negative presence within our personalities, Icons, and set the template for Iconic echoes ("You're no good") and Iconic reactions ("I am unworthy—I give up"). We have been programmed to limit ourselves to survival-oriented strategies, which include self-demeaning thoughts and self-defeating behaviors.

Of course, the severity of one's problem varies with the abusive nature of the environment that they survived. The child they were however, was so impressionable that the abusive comments, gestures, and behaviors that they were subjected to, from mild to severe, were stored in memory and are now triggered back into consciousness by the Icon, Iconic echo, and Iconic reaction that reside near the core of their personality. Often, especially as a consequence of a harsh and unfair environment, the child one was grows into an adult who spends hours of every day enduring negative messages from within that constantly remind them of their unworthiness. These Iconic echoes and reactions caution the person to remain silent, secretive, and ashamed, as these strategies historically kept them safe.

We are all impacted by the negative consequences of an abusive experience or experiences. It is the nature of the human condition. Most of us carry this burden in secret, not realizing that others are carrying it too.

A constant and pervasive message, with its twisted and irrational logic, rings in one's mind—telling them that risks are too great for a life that goes beyond just surviving, that somehow they are not worthy or capable of anything more than the meagre existence that they have. Often one does not realize that they have become transfixed with the strategies that allowed them to survive their youth. When they were in the first 15 years of life, they lived in a small world that was all that they knew. They only saw themselves on that stage with the players who lived there.

If you were born in a dysfunctional family, with violent parents who beat you, you presumed their violence and your victimization were fundamental aspects of everyday life. You may have developed violent emergency strategies out of necessity, strategies that are triggered unnecessarily in your efforts to solve the problems of your current life.

If you were born to play the part of a son or daughter of an alcoholic, you learned that skill set and the accompanying feelings that are connected to such a lifestyle. If you were used as the sex object of another, then you developed, out of necessity, the philosophy of the victim and the conclusion that the good life was never for you.

There are however, basic and undeniable truths about the human condition. We all have a longing to go beyond the need for personal survival. We all seek respect and fairness from our fellow human beings. We all long for love and compasion from a partner who will cherish us. We all need that sense of fulfillment that comes from a productive life. Unfortunately, the abusive nature of the environment where we were first placed is the measure of the power of the negative Icons that limit us. We will be miserable, frustrated, and condemned unless we find a means to extricate our physical and psychological selves from the place of our pain and from the power of the Iconic echoes and Iconic reactions we employed to survive in the past.

This is our problem; to break from that mental condition within, the omnipresent voice and power of the Icon. We have all been abused in some fashion, and it is important to acknowledge that abusive experience—first to ourselves and then to a trusted confidant. At least then we will understand the nature of the problem. There is an abusive voice within telling us lies about who we are.

▶ Part 2: Overcoming the shame

The first part of the problem is the abuse itself and its self-condemning aftermath. The second part of the problem is the shame and the fear of humiliation that hold you to the old solution you used to deal with the abuse, especially secrecy. Often you are so entrenched in your fight to maintain your survival strategies, especially keeping those deep core problems private, that you cling to a lifestyle that is psychologically destructive.

Before you enter therapy or counselling, you will be torn by two forces. The first is a desire to change the way you are and speak about your problems, current and past. The second is the unconscious belief that any shift in strategies to acquire that change will somehow be negative and may even lead to the death of something very important—the way you have always been, the way you have managed to survive. Before you begin counselling, you may fear that you will risk losing the essence of how you connect to the world, even if that connection is weak or dysfunctional. Even reading this book and processing this particular concept, may cause you to reflexively assume that if you were to change your strategies your integrity would be at risk.

In the logical part of your mind, as you read this, you may be able to finally convince yourself that you might begin to change by sharing those difficult and upsetting secrets of abusive experiences that you endured. Logically and correctly, you are thinking: "I will take the chance. I will risk humiliation, if that is what it takes, to change the way I think and feel about myself and my connection with life itself." At that moment of moving forward, there may be a counter urge to retreat as you fear that when you tell your story you will be embarrassed and ashamed at an intensity that will trigger thoughts of self-hatred, self-condemnation, and self-harm.

I want to reassure you that you do have the strength within to overcome the fear and shame that prevent you from speaking about those dark secrets. I encourage you to speak the truth, in spite of your fear that others will judge you as too weak to cope with the injustice you suffered. Before you disclose the sadness of the past, many of you will fear that, if you speak the unspoken, others will conclude that it was your fault all along, and your shame and fears will be confirmed. You, like all of us, fear that your shame will be exposed and you will feel humiliated. You fear that what you were told or encouraged to believe is actually true. ("He told me that I didn't deserve to be born in the first place. They told me I was stupid.")

As you read this book, you will be triggered to think about the injustices of the past and how they still haunt you. You will be reminded of the unfairness you endured. If you have read this far, mentally you are now in a better position to take the brave steps forward required for change to occur. The injustice you suffered and hid away will begin to rise to the surface of your consciousness. Its review in the context of the logic found on these pages will slowly prepare you to speak the truth out loud, to finally share secrets that have reverberated within but never without. This is the first step in defining the Iconic nature of your concerns: acknowledging to yourself the root cause of your problems and revealing them to another person whom you trust. If you have already taken this step with a counsellor, you will have found some relief, but there is more work to be done. Often the negative emotional morass and the bad habits of denigrating yourself that were set in place by the Iconic process remain. There is hope for this as well.

After your brave disclosure, the barriers remaining include the shame, embarrassment, and guilt attached to the problem. Your understanding and acceptance of these harmful elements within your psyche began formulation at the time of the injustice. These elements were conceptualized within the mindset of the younger person that you were then. Now, as a maturing adult, you are in a different situation. Now you can logically define the shame, embarrassment, and guilt as neither justified nor deserved; they are things that you can break through, discuss, redefine—and leave behind. Now you know, as you did not before, that the problems hidden behind those negative emotions need to be revealed and defined before you can find resolution within. This is the beginning.

The Solution

▶ Speaking to the Icon

In reality, the abusive person or experience from the past is not the primary problem. It is the memory of the injustice, what I have called the negative Icon, that is the primary problem. It is the mental representative of the person or the series of events that hurt you in reality, and now condemn you every day in your mind ("You are not good enough"). The survival strategies established at the time of the injustice, set in place to cope with a problematic mother, for example, led to an alignment with her and the development of an Iconic reaction, the self-condemning inner thought: "I now believe, as my mother said, that I am not good enough." As well, angry thoughts for the mother and the situation in which you found yourself at that time have also emerged.

It is not necessary to think these self-condemning thoughts anymore or carry anger for the injustices endured. We all know that thoughts of this nature are counterproductive to psychological health. These thoughts come from the haunting Iconic echo that continually reminds you of your unworthiness. This message, of course, is entirely false—a significant error in thinking. You are more than worthy! You have survived an horrendous upbringing or a terrifying/upsetting series of events. All that remains is the brainwashing from the past—the very negative Iconic echo that interferes with your efforts to find your journey in life.

There is as well a small, quashed voice within, your true voice. It is calling for you to establish and maintain a sense of personal integrity (self-acceptance and self-appreciation); to experience, reciprocate, and cherish love from another and; finally, to discover and develop an involvement, connection, and commitment to a meaningful life. This is the voice that you want to bring to the surface, a voice that needs to speak the truth about past injustice; a voice that will shut down the negative messages that resonate with the hurts from the past.

> **For deep personal change to be lasting and effective, this Iconic echo and the Iconic reaction have to be shut down. This is the underlying purpose of Iconic therapy.**

In therapy or counselling, then, you and your counsellor must first gain an understanding of the problem, not only as initially presented but also from its Iconic perspective. Once the Icon has been defined, then it must be dealt with directly. This is difficult, but with the right therapist, the process is straight forward.

▶ The first session

Generally, when you meet with your psychologist or counsellor, you will present the initial problem, for example, depression ("I just feel depressed all the time"). Although it is not the case for all types of therapy, for Iconic therapy the counsellor should begin by asking about your history so that your journey in life to this point can be assessed in a relatively comprehensive manner. Generally, the history-taking will reveal that you have endured abusive events in a number of different situations, where one traumatic event set up vulnerability for the next. For example, there could be mother abandonment, which leads to foster-home placement, where sexual abuse occurs. Then the low self-esteem that results from these two difficult situations leads to a poor selection of friends who live a high-risk lifestyle. Then one of the treasured friends dies tragically. These three events (mother abandonment, sexual abuse, death of a friend) each establish an Icon and the Iconic process. For successful therapy to occur, each Icon has to be dealt with directly. From the client's perspective, the problem may be perceived simply as depression. The therapist's perception of the problem addresses its deeper Iconic roots and, as well, the corresponding depression.

▶ A new way to think about your problem

Once the configuration of the personality and the presence of the Icons are understood by the therapist, then the Iconic theory in a simplistic form can be presented to you, the client, revealing the connection between the Icons and the accompanying Iconic echoes (images, feelings, hurtful comments) consistent with abandonment issues ("I don't want you; you're unlovable"), sexual abuse ("You are only good for one thing"), and tragic loss ("You are cursed; the people you love will die"). You will come to understand that you have personalized these condemning statements ("I'm unlovable; I'm not worthy") for survival purposes. These personalized messages have gained power and consolidation through the exponential repetitions brought on by the mental review of every situation that has been perceived as putting your survival and integrity at risk. These self-condemnations have established a strong presence within your personality. These messages have contributed in a significant manner to the feelings of depression that you have experienced and want to address in the counselling sessions.

Often, to complicate the matter, you choose to minimize the impact of past traumatic events and the power of the memories stored as Icons as this feel like a safe thing to do. In the previous example, the mother-abandonment Icon, the sexual-abuse Icon, and the death-of-a-friend Icon established a place in the personality. Each Icon generated negative images, upsetting feelings, and irrational conclusions, which continually reminded this client of their unworthiness. Further this client's mental efforts to minimize and discount the impact of the upsetting events were used as a coping strategy that initially allowed survival but is now counterproductive to therapy and must be set aside for progress to be made.

When you, as the client, finally share your history of mistreatment, the psychologist you see will often classify these messages, such as "I'm not good enough," as errors in thinking, cognitive distortions, and negative core beliefs. For example, when you reveal the inner message of "I'm unlovable," with the use of cognitive restructuring techniques, the psychologist or counsellor will suggest that this is not true, as in the world apart from the abusive environment, there is evidence to suggest that you possess numerous positive qualities. His or her comments, although helpful, do not shut down these inner thoughts that continue to haunt you. The counsellor may say it once: "It's not true; you *are* worthy." However, the Icon, feeding on the energy of the traumatic memory it represents, says it a thousand times: "You deserved the abuse you suffered."

Changing these negative thoughts is what therapy is all about. These thoughts will not change with one or two discussions wherein the faulty logic of the inner messages is pointed out. They have at their foundation powerful and traumatic moments in your life that at the time were perceived as life-threatening. The power of these life-threatening memoires is not easily set aside through logical analysis.

The underlying dynamic for therapeutic change does not rely on logic alone. Two and two does not always equal four in therapy. To begin, the relationship with the counsellor needs to be one of trust, a trust that the therapist will lead in a safe way to a place where healing will occur. A sense of alliance and partnership needs to be established, wherein both therapist and client are examining issues not only logically but with a shared sensitivity regarding the emotional impact of the suffering endured. It is the release and the emotional expression of these feelings of pain, suffering, and disrespect to a trusted confidant that is the first step in shutting down the Icon within. Penetrating and enduring insight ("I am worthy") only follows the experiencing and releasing of the entrenched and very painful feelings held within.

► The Icon must be attacked not only from a logical perspective but also on an emotional plane

Although you are initially reluctant, you finally agree with your therapist's conclusion. You are a person of worth. You agree that you no longer need to endure the Iconic process, the destructive negative thoughts. The negative Iconic echo and reaction soften for that moment in therapy. Unfortunately, during your next encounter with one of life's ongoing stressors—say, for example, a negative comment from your boss at work—it returns. The Iconic echo and its reaction return out of habit, the survival habit, energized by the Icon—that negative morass of emotion that lies deep within the recesses of your personality. Even the supportive and concerned comments from a trusted psychologist or cherished partner are diminished, often set aside by the negative power of the Iconic echo and its Iconic reaction. Your Iconic echo and Iconic reaction continue, for the most part, unscathed by all the logical therapy talk. The voices and the feelings of the Iconic echo come from your emotional centre and must be reached on an emotional plane in order to be stopped.

Then, if you trust the psychologist or counsellor enough, you will speak more deeply and more revealingly about past situations and further clarify your history. These revealing discussions will bring some relief, and your depression will lift somewhat and your anxiety will lessen, especially if this is the first revelation of the truth from previously endured abuse and unfairness. Next, you will need to accept that the problem is no longer your mother (if she, for example, was verbally or in other ways abusive towards you during your youth) but the constellation of memories, images, and voices that live in your mind and represent your mother—what I have called the mother-abandonment Icon with its accompanying negative Iconic echo and Iconic reaction.

In my experience, the Icon has to be confronted directly. This is the solution. There is no other efficient way. Attempting in therapy to discount with logical analysis, experiences that have at their base a deeply emotional component is like trying to talk someone out of being in love or talking them out of their fear of snakes. It is next to impossible and, in fact, may have a counterproductive effect, as the failed attempt adds to the error in thinking that you are just not good enough or smart enough to solve the problem. A more direct approach is required.

▶ Role play is required

A role play with the Icon is suggested—a role play in which you will confront the powerful Icon directly. The therapist or counsellor might suggest, for example, for a person struggling with an abusive mother-Icon: "It is very important to speak to your mother directly in a role play about how you feel. I will play the part of your mother, and she will speak through me." The role play will allow you a place and time for you to say, "I hated what you did to me" or "what you did hurt me."

Role play is the essential element of Iconic therapy. It will be your opportunity, as the client, to address your problem directly from a logical and, most importantly, an emotional level. It will allow you to express your anger, sadness, disappointment, frustration, and all of those feelings that have been repressed, sometimes for years. When you take on the role play you will find that these feelings want to be released, and most of you will be surprised at their intensity. As you begin, you will feel your emotions building within, and simultaneously you will feel a resistance to releasing those emotions. When you do express these feelings, you will experience a sense of release and lightness that will confirm that what occurred, the role play, was a good and necessary event in your healing journey. You will know that your true voice has finally spoken.

The therapist involved will need to know the principles of Iconic therapy so that he or she can play the part of the Icon. The therapist has to be skilled in this technique. It is important to ask the therapist whether he or she is familiar with the principles of Iconic therapy. It is a new approach to treatment and many therapists may not be aware of the techniques required in playing the part of the Icon. I describe the therapist's responsibilities for the role play in Appendix 1 at the end of this book.

For now, those of you who are exploring the possibility of change, you can prepare yourselves for the eventual role play by writing down what it is that you want to say to the person that hurt you. It is especially important to identify the *feelings* that you long to release.

The Resistance

Most of you will resist the role play. You may even refuse. As a therapist, I understand your reservation. You may not know why you refuse, other than it just does not feel right.

The role play is the door to a new life. When you go through that door, your concept of your abusive and painful experiences will change forever. You will discover a new understanding of yourself in relationship to the injustice you endured. You will begin to experience a quiescence (a quiet place) where the pain used to be. You will begin to sense brief moments of freedom and spontaneity: sensations you rarely felt before, except when you lost yourself in an addiction or, for some, when you were totally alone.

When you find the courage to take on the role play, you prepare yourself to expose and extinguish the frustration within. This is the time when you can confront those horrible comments from the Icon that you have endured so many times in your mind. This is your time to challenge the lies told about you ("you're no good") and finally, this is the time that you will put an end to the Iconic reaction within, that inner, self-defeating mantra ('I am not good enough to take the risk to be better") that keeps you safe but prevents you from reaching out for the full life. This is the therapeutic moment when your life can change. This is the moment when your voice will finally be heard.

With this type of reward waiting for you, one would think that you would stand eagerly on that bungee platform, knowing the jump will challenge your survival instincts but also knowing it will be safe. One would think that you would choose this leap to the freedom that comes with confronting the Icon directly. Finally, the truth will have been spoken and revealed in its emotional character. You will have leapt to the integrity that comes when you finally speak with your inner voice and separate yourself from the past that holds you. This will finally be a leap through and beyond that negative propaganda that has washed over you daily since the injustice began.

▶ The most difficult thing of all

But, like many, you will step back. It is extremely difficult to go beyond what you have always known. Your errors in thinking, practised for years, will flood your mind with rationalizations to protect the fragile version of yourself, which uses fear to keep you safe. You will hear yourself saying, "I can't do it," "I don't believe you [the therapist] and your approach will work," "I've solved these problems," 'I don't do role plays," "I don't want to risk crying." "I don't want to risk the shame I might feel," "I can't summon up the energy to do it"; and/or "I don't want to bring up those memories again. I don't know how I'll respond."

The power of the Icon and that negative voice within remains as strong as it was when those seeds were planted, often when you were a defenseless child. The primary aspect of the fear comes from the child within you; your inner child's perception of the problem, triggered and re-experienced many times over the years. This is the fear that you will be humiliated and shamed, as you were in your youth. You will also question your own ability to find words to attack or at least address the painful memories. Even though you have minimized that fear ("What happened wasn't that bad; it didn't scare me that much") and denied its continual presence ("I am over that"), the fear remains powerful. It is still there, lurking in the shadows, preventing action that moves toward change. This is the fear that prevents personal growth.

From an outsider's perspective, one would think that to speak to the injustice in the role play—where you address the mother, father, abuser, murderer, or suicided loved one—would not be particularly difficult, especially in a therapeutic situation where it is clearly all imaginary. But in most cases, it is very difficult. In reality, people avoid the role play because they not only still fear the power of the Icon but also fear what will happen when their feelings toward it are released.

When you say no to attempting the role play, the Icon wins again; the Iconic reaction, the inner thought, "I'm not worthy" continues. The secret thought within—"Don't do it, because it will lead to shame and humiliation"—wins the moment, and progress is stopped. You have become the battered victim, beaten down too many times with the negative voice within, with no strength and no will power left to contemplate escape even when the way out is there. It is too scary. It would be too emotional. It is too different from what you know. You may decide that it is better to live with the devil you know than with whatever is beyond.

To further complicate the matter, you might also fear that you will not be able to handle the intense anger that remains within you for the injustice endured. Your deep-seated anger has percolated, possibly for years. You fear its release might cause you to lose self-control to a level that you do not understand and do not want to risk. You suspect that if you do the role play, you might release powerful emotions that you had to set aside to survive the initial trauma(s). You may fear that you will become overwhelmed with the power of these repressed emotions ("If I did that, I would get so angry I would hit you!").

Although it is seldom acknowledged, another fear you will have is that of crying ("I've cried too much; I can't go through that again"). In part, at least, you will be intimidated by the emotional catharsis that you fear will occur within the therapeutic moment.

Do not condemn yourself for being afraid or reluctant. It is part of the healing journey. Be gentle with yourself. It is a tough journey. Understand why you resist. You need to remember, and your counsellor needs to know, that you are being asked to take on a role that you have seldom or never imagined possible. It is very difficult to confront and demand justice from one's mother, father, or abuser, or to ask "why" of the suicided loved one. Your reluctance will, of course, be respected. It is your right to say no. But you also need to understand that this therapeutic strategy is the way to break the hold of the Icon. It is how you will get control of your own mind. It is how you can take back the power that is rightfully yours. It is the first step to freedom—the freedom to speak for and feel for yourself. The fight for personal freedom is not an easy one, but it is a fight that you can win!

This is where the real therapy begins—this is why I hope, when you read this book and then meet with your psychologist or counsellor, you are ready to make this leap. It is not a leap of faith; it is a leap based upon the logic and evidence supporting this theory. If you are ready, nothing terrible will happen. There will only be tears, sadness, and anger—which are the honest expressions of who you are at a deeper level.

You will finally reconnect with your true self. This will be your moment to speak and feel the truth. The Icon within will hear your voice for the first time and will listen. The inner relationship between you and the Icon will change. The condemning voices and feelings will begin to diminish immediately upon completion of this therapeutic task. Finally, you will have a sense of resolution. Your personality, even with this difficult but brief effort, will begin to move forward beyond the pain and suffering of the past. You will feel different; you will feel lighter.

For those of you who doubt this process, I encourage you to take on the role play anyway. If you believe that you have solved all those problems from the past, then the role-play exercise will be easy, and it will be clear that no problem exists, or if it ever did, it has been resolved. However, this is seldom the case. The problem is still there 99 percent of the time, and your saying that it is not is just part of your (sometimes unconscious) reflexive denial strategy. Try the role play. Take the chance. Overcome your natural tendency to resist.

The connection with the Icon through the role-play exercise is usually genuine and powerful. It is as if you are talking directly to the abusive person, the perpetrator, or your mother, or father, or whomever it was that hurt you. Later, you might relate that it felt as if you were confronting the real person. This occurs approximately 80 percent of the time.

A smaller percentage comprises those clients who have detached somewhat from the emotions involved. Although they can enter the role play, their emotions are still somewhat removed. They may hold back their anger: "I didn't release all the anger; there is too much, and it would be too hard." With many of these disconnected individuals, another try at the role play at a later date may bring some resolution. Individuals who are extremely damaged may be able to do the role play but with a clear disconnect from deeper emotions that are buried too deep to recover. These people will require long-term therapy.

▶ Other alternatives

It has been asked, why not confront the mother, the father, or the abuser directly, rather than through role play? Generally, this is discouraged. If the person is to be confronted directly, it should be done after the role play. Remember, the Iconic echo has been reverberating for years, laying in negative message after negative message, while at the same time building up strong resentment and anger for the injustices—which have been reviewed mentally many times. Often, the amount of resentment or anger or sadness is beyond the victim's capacity to express and release in an appropriate or acceptable fashion. Role play in a controlled setting, with the therapist as the controller, will allow for the safe release of the toxic emotions held within. Once the role play has been completed and the accompanying insight it brings has been processed, then the victim may be ready to confront directly. Even then, a direct confrontation may not be wise.

A role play with the psychologist or counsellor is often better than confronting the perpetrator directly for a number of other reasons. For starters, the abusive person may no longer be alive or their whereabouts may not be known and a direct confrontation is not be possible. Second, upon confrontation, the horrible truth that the mother/father/abusive person would have to face may be overwhelming for them—a truth that she or he cannot live with. After such a confrontation, she or he may choose to terminate the relationship, a relationship that you may want to maintain even though it has been filled with dysfunction. Finally, if the abusive person is brought into the therapy and is confronted, that person brings with them all of their abusive ways of relating, their errors in thinking and their own Iconic echo. In part, at least, they may attempt to justify their problematic behavior and, in doing so, continue to act in an abusive fashion. If they have been abusive in the past they may continue to relate that way in the present. In some cases they may refuse to listen; they may shout you down; they may even become violent. That is how they have always been and unless they have embarked on their own journey of healing, this is how will continue to be.

For a number of reasons, then, it is often best for the psychologist or counsellor to portray the abusive Icon in role play. He or she will be able to create a safe, relatively non-threatening environment for you to let go and release the pent-up feelings that you have been holding back for so long.

Icons form within all of us, initially serving as survival mechanisms. These Icons limit future personal growth. In what you have read to this point, I have emphasized abuses from childhood. However, abusive and unfair events from the recent past can also begin the Iconic process (i.e., self-condemning thoughts). Here are examples of experiences, past and more current, that often lead to the formation of Icons within that prevent growth:

- parental abandonment, neglect, and mistreatment;
- sexual assault, sexual abuse, and sexual innuendo;
- physical and verbal assault, domestic violence;
- witnessing or being exposed to the death of others and/ or experiencing or witnessing near-death events, including wartime traumatic experiences;
- the sudden death by murder, suicide, or accident of loved ones;
- other negative environmental stressors (at home, at work, in the community).

These are the extreme examples upon which this treatment approach has been developed. The treatment approach works equally as well for the milder versions of all of the above. Let us begin by examining predominant forms of abuse and the specific strategies required to separate from one's history of past abuse.

CHAPTER 6
Coping with Parental Abandonment and Abuse

To my father:

I cannot even think where to begin to tell you how I feel about what you did to our family. It has been years since I have seen you and since you left ... You tried taking me, too, but I ended up saying no. I couldn't have left Mom alone with Timothy and Chris ... You made a bad decision to leave. I believe that you are a coward for leaving your family. I blame you, and because of you I have no father ... I didn't know it then, but I used to lash out at the world because I was mad at you for leaving us ... Am I not good enough to be your son, or is it that Mom wasn't a good enough mom? ... I feel like a coward because of you ... I don't know what it is that I fear so much about coming to terms with you leaving ... I always feel like I'm not good enough.

The Threatened Child Struggles for Survival

Parental abuse or abandonment is one of the most devastating traumatic experience (or series of experiences) that occurs, forcing the development of an extreme survivor-oriented personality and a powerfully negative Icon within. Our parents were human and they made mistakes in their relationships with us. They said things they should not have said. Even if they were not physically abusive, one stinging and negative verbal comment can plant the seeds, establishing an Iconic echo in a sensitive child and triggering a survival response that will reverberate for years.

Powerful authority figures—including parents, teachers, pastors, dance instructors, sports coaches and policemen—at times do things that are unfair or abusive, with long-lasting negative consequences. Often unknowingly, sometimes with good intentions, they place the negative Icon in the landscape of the developing personality of the young child. All energy within that personality begins to flow in relationship to that negative Icon. As the survival strategy is self-reinforcing—that is, the victim of even the mildest abuse continues to survive (and escape anxiety) with the use of the almost-reflexive survival strategies, necessary or not—the power of the Icon within increases. Its negative presence is continually reinforced, acknowledged, and accepted as legitimate. Feared potential perpetrators of abuse are generally avoided, and avoidance becomes the primary survival strategy. With each execution of this defensive and self-protecting strategy, the menacing Icon within becomes stronger.

The Limiting Nature of Negative Icons

The negative Icons that develop within one's personality have the power to destroy or extremely limit one's personal development. The parent-abandonment/parent-abuse Icon is one of the most damaging and long lasting. The approach in dealing with this particular type of Icon will be described below. This will assist you in understanding the therapeutic mindset required to move forward in your healing journey.

An extreme example will be used to explain the development of the parent-abandonment Icon. For efficiency, the abusive mother will be used to illustrate this aspect of the theory. Father abuse as demonstrated in the quote at the beginning of this chapter is also very painful, and it too is dealt with using the same approach.

In this example, imagine that the mother uses crack cocaine or alcohol excessively. She initially neglects and later abandons her child. The child, from his or her self-centered perspective, presumes the following: "Mom chose crack (or alcohol) over me; I must be a bad person. I upset Mom; that's why Mom does crack. I must be unlovable. If I was good, she would stop."

The child strives to impress the mother by being good. The child believes that chances for survival are improved if her mother will care for and nurture her. The mother, overwhelmed with her own problems, fails to notice the child's effort. The child perceives the situation in the simplistic, black-and-white thinking style typical of a child: "I guess I was so bad there's no hope, but I will keep trying."

▶ An Iconic echo develops to cope with the Icon within

In the end, the child's failed efforts to obtain a sense of safety, security, and nurturing provided by a loving mother have evolved as follows. First, she mentally hears her mother's voice repeating what was heard in reality, "don't bother me now" or "I wish you were never born," often said in a moment of exhaustion. The child fears abandonment and processes the information as follows:

> I am not worthy of my mother's love. If others knew the truth, they would know that I am less than them, that somehow I am a despicable person. If they find out, I will be humiliated. It's bad enough being a despicable person; I just don't want others to know.

The mother, because of her own problems, eventually abandons the child to welfare services. The child continues efforts to win the mother back, to increase chances for the nurturing required to enhance survival. At the same time, the rejecting mother-memory (the mother Icon) echoes within with all the attached images and thoughts, especially the thought first heard as "You are an unlovable person" and later processed as "I am an unlovable person."

The mother in this example is the primary power force in the life of this child. Her presence and her actions are stored within the child's personality as an Icon that constantly repeats rejecting mother-messages that were first heard in everyday exchanges with the mother. Years pass, and these exchanges are reviewed mentally by the young person until, as a troubled adult he or she attends a psychologist, still carrying the negative messages, the Iconic echoes, caused by childhood experiences.

While the mother in this example is perceived as overwhelming in her power, the Icon that represents the mother within the personality is experienced as a vaguer and more diffuse form that inexplicably triggers feelings of unworthiness. The logical connection between the mother Icon and the feelings of unworthiness is often lost. The unworthiness is experienced as a natural, inherited and unalterable state. The personality has been shaped by these circumstances to continue with an unconscious striving for the mother's love. The Icon within, the mother Icon, is sending messages that the personality responds to, but the messages over time are altered somewhat, consistent with the child's view of ideal survival— namely, winning the mother back. The messages begin with the mother's voice: "If you are good, I will return. If you are good, I will love you." Then these messages are rationalized by the child to form an Iconic echo: "Mom is the source of life. Mom is all I know. She is all knowledge. She is right. She rejects me. I must have been bad; I'm a really bad person." Eventually the never ending mantra within becomes disconnected from the mother Icon to be experienced as a permanent personal quality, the Iconic reaction: "I'm unlovable. I'm despicable. I will try to be good."

In my experience as a psychologist, I have met numerous clients who suffer from the early traumatic experience of parental abandonment. The extreme version of this core problem is often manifested in criminal ways, which will be explained later. The less extreme version of the problem is manifested in a life fraught with inner self-defeating messages, which I strongly believe can be stopped. Once the nature of the Iconic problem has been revealed, then the deeper-level therapy can begin. The negative mother Icon or father Icon within has been contaminating the personality with negative messages: "You are not good enough to love." These messages are personalized by the victim: "I am not good enough to love." An inner life inundated with this type of propaganda is self-destructive. It makes every day functioning more difficult as, with each triggering stimulus in the environment, the self-defeating messages reverberate. The person looks away from the problems of everyday life that need to be addressed in an attempt to find safety. These efforts to find safety reduce feelings of anxiety and fear and quiet the Iconic echo and reaction. The problems of daily life however take on a more frightening aura and are often avoided or left unresolved. Personal failures result which add to one's feelings of worthlessness.

▶ The role of mothers

Mothers have special and unique responsibilities that have a profound impact on the developing personalities of their children. When a mother comes up short and does not provide the love and nurturance required by the child, very serious psychological damage results. Mothers, you are loved and needed so much, but when your love is withheld, the rejection can be devastating. It has the potential to cause the greatest psychological pain one can experience. Our ability to trust and feel safe in the world is strongly rooted in this mother-daughter or mother-son relationship. When it is abusive, the impact is severe and potentially life-altering.

I want to be clear about this. Most mothers are wonderful people. We loved them and feel forever in debt for their efforts to raise us as children. The mother-child relationship has an almost sacred quality and is the first and most important connection for the child with the world. The mother's loving efforts serve as a template for the child when the child becomes a parent. It is the nature of the human condition that, as children, we are dependent upon the care of our parents for a long time, especially our mothers. My words fall far short in describing the importance and special quality of this relationship.

But let's be fair. Mothers are human. They make mistakes. Their upbringings were far from perfect and may have engendered beliefs, attitudes, and behaviors that caused them to be over-controlling, too quick to judge, or the reverse—too soft and too permissive. Possibly they endured postpartum depression that left them temporarily unable to nurture and love their children. Maybe they mistakenly left their loved children with the wrong babysitters. Maybe they married for a second time out of desperation, and the stepfathers had issues. Maybe they were victimized by abusive husbands who diminished their abilities to parent. Maybe they were abused themselves and they carry haunting Iconic imagery and verbiage that holds them back from connecting with and loving their children. All of these circumstances can affect mothers and lead them to treat their children in such a way that Iconic echoes are developed within the children that compromise and limit them as young adults.

Many of you will have issues with the way you were raised by your mothers or your fathers, but to be fair, I have not heard their sides. From my perspective, it is not prudent to judge another's behavior without knowing the whole story. In general, I am primarily interested in what happens when the mother-daughter or mother-son, or father-daughter or father-son relationship goes wrong from the client's perspective. If change is to occur, it is essential that the psychologist understand how you recall the damaging parent-child relationship. Often this can be obtained quite quickly by having you describe the most painful and most appreciated memories from your relationships with each of your parents. Often, one or two of these memories symbolize the heart of the parent-child relationship. The landscape of your personality generally finds its basic formation in your relationship with your mother and your father.

Mild Forms of Abuse from Parents

For those of you who experienced milder forms of parental abuse you may develop the strategy "I'll be a really nice person" as a means of coping. This may be your reaction to the abusive child-rearing philosophy mentioned earlier, wherein children are to be seen but not heard, where backtalk is met with punishment, and where you were treated like a servant and required, in an excessive manner, to clean, babysit, and do chores.

When abusive tactics are used to train children to be nice to everyone, to be obedient and to not discern between good adults and bad, they later become adults who are not prepared to defend their boundaries when they are mildly violated. It follows that even mild abuse may lead to this type of personality style, "I'll be a really nice person." *Niceness* is then used in an extreme fashion as a means of warding off deeply rooted fears that abuse or disrespect will reoccur. At the same time, however, with their niceness and their victim-like personality, they are attracting abusers. If you have developed this style of survival, you will be vulnerable to taking on the role of caregiver and doing almost anything to please a needy friend, while at the same time neglecting your own needs and risking what little remains of your integrity.

Some of you who have been raised in relative stability have endured cruel comments and mild forms of verbal abuse. One stinging comment made by a mother or father during a moment of frustration can trigger an Iconic echo that will cause a long-lasting inner reverberation during the important developmental stages of the personality. For example, a mother might say in anger "sometimes I wish you were never born" or "you were the biggest mistake of my life!" Even though stated only once or twice, even though not truly meant, these types of comments are perceived as a threat to existence and may reverberate within the child's mind and the Iconic reaction begins: "Mom never really loved me as a child" or "She could only love me on the good days." Then Iconic reactions form solutions: "Maybe if I am extra good, Mom will appreciate me. I need her love to survive." When the source of the problem is left unspoken for years and, for the most part unresolved, the following conclusions may form: "I know I can't trust my mother's love; possibly I'm unlovable. I'll try to overcome that problem by being really nice to everyone; I will be extra lovable. But, to protect myself, I will not get too close to anyone. I will even fool myself and blame my loving partner for his lack of attractiveness."

When it is your turn to make and establish a long-term commitment to the family where you are the parent, the Iconic echo of "You were a mistake; you were never wanted; you were never loved" may trigger harmful Iconic reactions such as "Love and closeness will lead to betrayal; don't commit too much; don't commit to family; don't commit to children; deep love will meet with pain and rejection."

The opposite can occur as well. You may develop into a parent who strives to please all in the family, including the children, in an excessive way: "I will please you; then you will love me; I'll try to be perfect in my relationship with you; that will lead to the love I have been denied. Finally, I will feel accepted." This effort confuses the children, who long for clear and safe boundaries in their efforts to define themselves in the early stages of their journey to adulthood.

When one speaks this error in thinking out loud (e.g., "Don't commit to family") in a therapy session or with a trusted friend, its validity will be denied and this type of Iconic reaction will lose some of its power. If this memory is never addressed outside the psyche however, never mentioned in a conversation with another, it remains to continually resonate within one's inner life. Like waves pounding on the shore, it poisons one's effort to truly commit to their partner, their family, and to the journey in life they truly desire. If that Iconic reaction is attacked in a role play, one of the key exercises in the Iconic approach, that error in thinking will be, for the most part, totally set aside, and the person is then able to reach out with a strong and more committed effort to strive for the essence of a life that previously had seemed unavailable.

Mothers and fathers make mistakes in their efforts to raise their children. They are human, not perfect, and they say hurtful things that should never have been said. It happens. If it has happened to you, then it is your problem. Sure, your mother or your father had a lot to do with it, but let's not blame them. They may have had issues with their parents or another caregiver, and what they did was all they knew how to do. All of your efforts to blame your parents or to change them generally will not work for you. Hanging on to the strategy of blaming your parents will leave you with feelings of self-centered satisfaction, but attached will be long-term frustration, anxiety, and lack of connection not only with your mother or father but with relationships in general.

If your problem has its source as a mild version of parent-abandonment, it may impact you on two levels. First, your own ability to be a parent may be tainted. When you attend the psychologist you may present the problem from this perspective ("I struggle to be the loving parent I want to be.") This problem however, is a manifestation of the deeper problem, the problems you had with your own parents and the resulting negative Icon (the memories of mild abuse from you mother or father), the Iconic echo (the inner repetition of the punishing parent's voice saying "I wish you were never born") and the Iconic reaction (the processing of that voice to your own conclusion, "I am unlovable"). Thus the deeper problem ("I am unlovable and therefore cannot be a loving mother") has to be dealt with first. Taking self-improvement courses on how to be a good parent or how to be a good partner to your spouse is like swimming upstream against the Iconic reaction, while it repeats: "I am unlovable and I won't trust others in love relationships because they will find out." This type of inner dialogue has to be shut down before you can move beyond the inner conflict to being a good mother. Many therapists will, like you, get tangled up in the presenting problem. They will teach you skills on how to be more loving or how to be better at setting boundaries, but they will not get to the deeper issue: the betrayals you have suffered and the Iconic echoes and reactions that remain. That is where you should begin.

Once you have arrived at the stage where you can see two dimensions to the problem, you will be gaining insight into possible next steps. Typically at this stage you will cling to the rationalization that even though the Iconic echo ("you are unlovable") is related to the problem, it is not essential to address it. What happened in the past, you will argue, is unchangeable. You may even refuse to take any other stance, saying something like this:

> Why talk about that? My father had his problems [or my mother had hers]. They will never admit or apologize for what they did. That will never change. It is all in the past. I refuse to go there to deal with my issues of today. It is too upsetting.

This is the denial, the minimization, the rationalization—the propaganda from within that will stop your development.

For the psychologist or the counsellor, this is the hardest part. It is his or her role to help you realize that you will have to go to that depth. This is where the deeper healing will begin. Often I am left with my last-stand effort to take on your well-established rationalization: "My father (or mother) will never change and never apologize." In my role as psychologist, I will say the following:

> I do not believe that your father has to change for you to find your way in life. You do not have to have an

apology from your father [or mother, or brother, or abuser] for you to grow and develop, to carry on in your journey to be the person you want to become. If you believe that you must have an apology, is it fair that you have to wait to get it before you can move on with your life? If your father died, would that prevent you from being the person you want to be because you couldn't get your apology? No. You can find personal growth and development in spite of the difficult things your father did.

With a skilled psychologist or counsellor, if you are open enough or courageous enough to try the strategies offered within this theory, you will need to begin with your description of the painful events you endured as a child in the problematic relationships of your youth. Together you and your therapist will try to gain a perspective on why your parent would have responded in the manner that they did. Finally, as noted above, you will need to find the never-revealed feelings and the right words to communicate with the father and/or mother symbol, the Icon, in the role play. This will stop the Iconic process. This will change your personality. This will open you to love and a deeper connection with the world in general.

The Extreme Manifestation of the Mother (or Father) Abandonment Icon

If you are a very troubled adult who experienced extreme mother abandonment (or father abandonment) as a youth and struggled through to find survival, the Icon-generated errors in thinking are generally more severe in their condemning aftermath. The thoughts and images generated by the Icon permeate your personality and may serve as the foundation for a variety of maladaptive coping strategies that could include the beginnings of criminal conduct.

This type of extreme Iconic reaction may contain a constellation of attitudes and behaviors that are attempts to find love and attachment with unconventional and often antisocial strategies.

In extreme circumstances, abandonment by a parent or by both parents often puts in place a powerful negative Icon that energizes strategies that are oriented to acquire, appropriate, or even steal the love given to others in the form of possessions. Those suffering this extreme manifestation, or coping strategy, unknowingly long for certain material possessions as symbols of parental love never received. Stealing these material possessions, or acquiring them illegally or immorally, is a coping strategy for the very desperate, wherein the stolen products serve as substitutes for nurturing and love never obtained. The excessive acquisition of material possessions, even stolen goods, demonstrates to the damaged psyche that survival can be managed, albeit poorly, without the basic nurturing and love from the parenting figure.

For those of you who suffered extreme damage as a consequence of traumatic parenting, you have been enduring an almost-overwhelmingly negative Iconic echo, which has been lying to you as it says:

> You are unlovable, not even worthy of a mother's or father's love. Everyone who discovers the nature of your unworthiness will come to detest you. Keep your unworthiness secret. Others will not give you love. Others, when they know, will give you nothing.

I want you to remember that this Iconic echo is not true. You are lovable and worthy of the respect of others. I know that the mere words in this book will not stop the Iconic echo that has been forged within your mindset. Unfortunately, because you are carrying this extremely damaging parent-abandonment Iconic echo, it is quite possible that you will turn to the hoarding and worshipping of possessions as compensation. Some of you will be destined to steal the possessions of others—possessions that symbolize the love you have never realized or received.

In the extreme cases (most of you are not at this stage), you may even steal the life spirit from another by destroying them or controlling them. When this condition is at its worst, you can manage to live in response to the Iconic echo with an Iconic reaction that is extreme. Your alignment with the abuser has become complete. "I don't ever need to deeply connect with anyone. I will find pleasure in the toys I steal, in the thrills I arrange, in the people I control."

At your worst, you may find pleasure in hurting others as an expression of your anger for the way your life has unfairly evolved. An example of an extreme Iconic reaction might include thoughts as follows:

> I hate all who remind me of my unworthiness, of the rejection I have suffered. I hate all of you who got the love I should have received but never did. My hatred is so strong that I will find pleasure in destroying those who trigger my unexamined rage. If I die in the process, I don't care.

The worst-case scenario in the mother and/or father abandonment scenario is that you take on the qualities of the abuser you detest.

Psychologists often speak about the splitting of the personality in an effort to cope with problems. At one time, there was a diagnosis termed Multiple Personality Disorder, wherein a person could be diagnosed with having two or more personalities. (The term has been renamed Dissociative Identity Disorder.) The splitting-of-the-personality analogy is an interesting way of conceptualizing one's development. For mild parent-abandonment issues, a conflicting split in the personality develops: "I am lovable; I can succeed" versus "I am unlovable; all my efforts will lead to failure." From the Iconic perspective, the negative Icon lives and feeds the "I am unlovable" side of the divide, with this message reverberating throughout the entire personality when under stress. One is capable of living within both of these mindsets at the same time, as well as completely in one or the other, depending upon stressors in the environment. This is what occurs with most parent-abandonment issues, the energy force on each side of the divide being a function of the negative message the child received and continues to experience through the Iconic echo. Those children who have been totally abandoned are vulnerable to having their entire personalities separate from their longing for connection with others, leaving them wholly on the dark side and in a position to steal and strike out at others with no remorse. They feel totally justified in harming those they do not know—and they truly know and care for very few.

Many of you will have suffered some form of parental abandonment or betrayal, but not of the extreme variety. Parents are far from perfect, and their imperfections are communicated in their relationships with their vulnerable and defenseless children. Many of us have been raised by parents who suffered from addiction problems, often alcohol. During the moments of drunkenness and drug abuse of your parents you, as a child, developed strategies to cope. These strategies involved taking on the inner belief that you were part of a family system that had been poisoned. In part, at least, you took on the belief that somehow you added to the problem that pushed your parent(s) to rely on alcohol or drugs. In some fashion, you believed you were not good enough as a person to help out. As well, you may have concluded that you were weak when you did not stand up to the wrongdoing perpetrated, for example, upon you, your mother and your siblings by your father.

The inner thoughts that you are weak and cowardly quite possibly remain with you. Of course, these thoughts are based on faulty logic. The truth is, your parents just had problems. They were human, and they suffered—just as you are suffering—with inner torment. You do not have to carry the inner belief that the problems in your family are entirely your fault or were your responsibility to resolve. You do not have to live with the error in thinking that, because you did not stand up to an abuser when you were ten years old or still in your youth, you are weak or cowardly. You did the best you could to manage your survival. These errors in thinking that you were weak or worthless or cowardly are wrong! Unfortunately and tragically they now block your potential to be all you can be, to actualize your true self. I encourage you to bring these concerns, your abusive experiences as a young person to a therapist or psychologist who understands the Iconic impact. By following the strategies discussed below, you will quiet that inner voice that continually repeats the lie that you are not worthy.

Do not let the parent-abandonment Icon destroy you. Your parents had problems, and their inability to be nurturing in their relationship with you, hurt you. But the truth is that a beautiful spirit lies within you. You are worthy of the full life. You are worthy of taking on, first, your healing journey, and then, the journey to the rest of your life, wherein you will find personal fulfillment.

Here are encouraging words from one client who could see her healing journey ahead; let these words work for you, as well.

I am here to offer each of you hope. Hope that whatever decisions you choose you have support and no judgment. For we are all on our own journey, and on our journey there will be times when we will meet a crossroad, and life-changing decisions will have to be made.

What I write is to offer support and understanding. Through Courage of Women, I was, and still am, able to face my sexually abusive past. My experiences with abortions, birth, and healing from those circumstances have brought this letter and my wisdom for all of you. For each of you, I offer: my heart to empathize; my shoulder for tears; my eyes for compassion; my words for comfort; my hands to steady you; and my legs for pillars of strength for you if you need a safe place to fall.

CHAPTER 7
Coping with the Icon That Forms in Response to Sexual Abuse

My journey started in Wisconsin, when I was 15 years old. I was waiting alone to be picked up by some summer-camp counsellors. My parents had dropped me at a motel on their way to get some treatment for my dad's cancer, thinking I was old enough to take care of myself.

That afternoon I went for a swim in the pool. It was suppertime and all the families with kids were going in. Soon, everyone had left but me and an older man of about 30.

He kept swimming near me and talking. It was easy conversation, and I—being a naïve child—thought nothing of it. He walked me back to my room to "protect me" and offered to check my room to make sure it was safe.

He checked the room and then sat on the bed, patting beside him as he called me over. He rubbed my leg as he talked to me. The next thing I knew, he was on top of me on the floor between the beds. I remember his smell and his taste as he took my innocence. I've hated the smell of Old Spice ever since.

When he was done with me, he made me take a bath, and he sat and washed me. He talked gently, as if nothing had even happened. I was scared and ashamed, and I felt so guilty for being so stupid. But most of all I just felt numb.

Once I was clean, he got up and left. I couldn't move. I stayed in that bath until the next morning when the counsellors came to pick me up. They were mad that I wasn't ready. All I remember was shutting down my emotions. I look back and realize that my emotions have stayed that way all these years.

I pushed those feelings to the back of my mind and left them there. In their place, I wore a mask. That mask showed appropriate emotions, but I felt nothing inside. I still wear the mask often.

For years, I struggled with the feeling of never being good enough. Everything in my life seemed to be a struggle to be "good enough" at something. When one thing wasn't enough, I tried being good at everything.

The sad part was, I never did it for me. I always needed everyone's approval, and I became a people pleaser.

One day, about five years ago, a very good friend of mine made an observation that was right on the money. She told me her story of childhood rape, and for the first time in 20 years, I told my story.

She encouraged me to seek help for my trauma. To be honest, I had never thought of it like that. I started trying. I found that I just couldn't find therapy for my situation. They all wanted to fix the stubborn, general one-man-show attitude but not the cause of the attitude.

When Dr. Pugh suggested Courage of Women, I thought, "Okay, one more try." You have to be willing to heal, and you have to be willing to do a little work. I couldn't talk the first day in group, but I found my voice the next time.

The Sexual-Abuse Icon

The traumatic impact of being sexually assaulted or sexually abused generally results in the development of extreme survivorship strategies. If you are one of those individuals who have been sexually abused and kept it a secret, you know how seriously this abuse has impacted your development as a person. When you keep this secret, you harbor the shame, too. Any thought or effort to discuss with others what occurred is met with tremendous internal resistance. Even reading these words now brings your fears of exposure and re-victimization to the surface. These fears lie within your personality, initially placed to protect you. But now, years later, there is part of you that remains frightened, apprehensive, and angry deep within. This aspect of your personality can be triggered by certain stressors in the environment and this vulnerability as well, adds to your concerns.

When you read about your fears on these pages, and your anxiety increases, do not be afraid. I am on your side, and I want to remind you that healing *can* occur. There *is* a way through. Like most therapists, I would be honoured to help you. I would be privileged to speak to you the truth: the shame of your sexual abuse is not yours. I can help reduce or possibly eliminate the shame, fear, and anger that have lingered since the abuse occurred.

If you have been sexually abused, stop reading for a moment and take a deep breath. I say this to take the focus away from you and your personal pain for a moment. Let us take this time to reflect on how you can prepare for your healing journey and overcome the aftermath of the sexual abuse that was so unfairly perpetrated upon you.

Many of the uninformed, especially those who have never been sexually abused, have little understanding of the impact of a sexual abuse. After this type of experience, one's concept of safety and trust is severely damaged. Fear, guardedness, and shame find a place deep within the psyche and these feelings emit negative energy within that can linger for a lifetime. This negative energy is extremely counterproductive to personal growth.

Of course, the severity of the impact is different for each victim. However, for the most part, the damage is significant and life-altering. As with parental abandonment, splitting of the personality occurs, but the difference with sexual abuse is that the world was perceived as a relatively safe place up until that point. In most cases the child felt loved and supported by parents, family, and friends. Sexual abuse alters these feelings, leaving the victim feeling damaged and unlovable, carrying an unspeakable secret too horrible to reveal. Even though family and friends remain supportive, the victim's ability to reach out and trust in their comfort and support may have been so compromised by the abuse itself that their ability to re-connect is lost. Thus, that sense of personal security and self-acceptance, that inner belief that 'I'm okay—I'm lovable," is extinguished. It may never be rekindled, at least not with the same level of self-assurance. However, with the strategies in this book, there is hope—and even better, there is renewal.

When sexual abuse occurs the personality fractures. The feelings of horror, anger, sadness, guilt, and shame are separated from the primary personality. These feelings are generated as a consequence of the sexual abuse, but for survival purposes, they often cannot be dealt with in a healthy fashion at the time of the abuse. They separate from the primary part of consciousness that relates directly to the everyday reality of life. These feelings coalesce to form the Icon and the Iconic echo and establish a negative energy that emits messages to the primary personality. These messages resonate with the thoughts, feelings, and perceptions experienced at the time of the abuse and developed following the abuse. They resonate not only to process what happened or what continues to happen, but also in an effort to ward off future abuse.

If you were a victim of sexual abuse, it is typical that at the time you were being abused, you were smaller and weaker than your abuser(s). In this position of weakness and vulnerability, you most likely used silence and compliance as a means of survival. Of course, the one positive aspect of the abuse experience is that you survived it. But the abusive experience was, for most of you, so horrible or so confusing that you have been left with maintaining emergency strategies for survival, which you use almost reflexively in your everyday life. You may often call upon the strategies of compliance and silence when you feel threatened or upset. If these do not work, then you are left with your fallback position: extreme anger and even violence. These strategies (i.e., silence, compliance, anger) generally will not lead to the type of success you want and deserve when used in everyday life. To add even more confusion to the sexual abuse scenario, there may have been occasions when you were being abused where you experienced pleasurable feelings. These feelings as well add to the shame that you feel. Often during the abusive events, you experienced and perceived condemning attitudes, statements, and behaviors from the abuser. When the abuse ended you were left with his mental representative, the Icon, with the echoed reminders you hear within: "You're deserving of this abuse; you are worthless; you should be ashamed; you should remain silent." These feeling-statements continue to resonate within your personality, even though they are not true.

The typical survival approach, compliance and secrecy, increases your chances for survival. You most likely will continue with this mindset long after the abuse ends, as the emergency survival strategies you developed were reinforced, over-learned, well-practiced, and consolidated during and following the abuse. Connected to this mindset are self-condemning feelings that may be strengthened if, when you first speak about your abuse, you are either not believed or silenced.

When I work with women and men who have been sexually abused and then not believed, I often see damaged and broken individuals who carry the belief: "My life has been destroyed by the sexual abuse." This powerful inner conviction is accompanied by the thought "I can never recover." Let me assure you, this conclusion is not true. There is recovery in the strategies explained below.

If you have been sexually abused, you are vulnerable to the use of drugs or alcohol to separate yourself from these overwhelming feelings of disgust and loss. As a consequence, two layers of abuse often evolve: the sexual abuse itself and the self-inflicted addiction used to cope with that abuse.

In some cases strategies are developed that involve an effort to deny or minimize what happened. You will try thoughts such as "I'll just pretend it didn't happen" or "I'll erase it from my mind" or "I'll act as if it didn't happen." I have never seen this strategy work, but to be fair, I remind myself that maybe I am only seeing the clients for whom the strategy did not work. As well, the strategy may work for a period of time but later, when under stress or when triggered by something similar in its threatening nature, the fears, anxieties and self-condemnations re-appear, as strong as they were in the first place.

It is in the nature of our humanness to speak about and verbally mediate the impactful events we experience. To be able to organize these past events in terms of verbal constructs allows us to understand at another level, in another dimension—the verbal/cognitive dimension—what has occurred. When you speak about what occurred, you are taking the first step toward shutting down the voice of the condemning Icon within. This is necessary in order to regain control of your inner life. When you disclose and then discuss your sexual abuse, you take ownership of your previously minimized or denied history. When you overcome the secrecy, you begin to experience another dimension of personal integrity. You discover that you are finding your voice.

The Fear of Being Re-traumatized

There are psychologists who take the stance that you should not speak about the sexual traumas you have experienced, as it could potentially re-traumatize you. This viewpoint suggests that, when speaking about the sexual abuse, you will be triggered to return to the trauma scene as if it were happening again. I have dealt with over 500 sexually abused, traumatized victims, and not one was re-traumatized in the sense that they were transported back totally to the traumatic event. Many of these clients became very upset, but all managed to get through the emotional upheaval and symbolically face the perpetrator of the abuse. All of those who tried the strategies that will be described in this book came out the other side reporting that they felt stronger. They believed that their issues had been identified at an emotional level and felt relieved that these issues had finally been addressed and, to a significant extent, resolved. They believed they could now leave them behind and move on with the rest of their lives.

To be fair, some dropped out of the therapy program before trying what was recommended. They did not make any progress, but at the same time, they were not re-traumatized. I believe they feared that the emotional expression required for progress would overwhelm them. The therapeutic-intervention strategies presented in this book are structured to avoid overwhelming the participants.

On another point, regarding the fear of re-traumatization, I explained this concept to one client. She related that this was a fear for her but not an overwhelming one. She stated that she had relived the traumatic event many times in her mind, often on a daily basis. It was always unsettling. She was quick to point out, however, that she could manage reliving it as a difficult therapeutic exercise, it if it would be constructive in her healing efforts. Her goal was to stop having this memory of trauma so easily triggered into the forefront of consciousness. In Iconic therapy, the client is encouraged in controlled conditions, to confront the Icon symbolically, so that they can alter or to add to their response within the memory of the trauma. This will lead to changing the mental imagery and memory traces of the traumatic event.

In addition, I believe that it is damaging when a therapist takes the position that you should never speak about a trauma as it may be too upsetting or possibly re-traumatizing. If you are advised to never speak about a trauma, then you are left with the view that you must continue to exist with this terrible sense of anxiety that is easily triggered by the stressors in your life. If this don't-talk-about-it strategy is used, you begin to believe that you will never be normal and never get past this horrible event. I believe being told, "Don't talk about it; it may overwhelm you," is destructive. It takes away your longing for resolution. It takes away your hope for a sense of peace within. As well, the don't-talk-about-it strategy may reinforce the thought that the trauma is too full of shame to speak about, and it follows that somehow you are a shameful person. You may be left with the thought: "If the therapist can't speak about it, then who can?" It is very sad if you conclude that the secret must continue to fester within. In my opinion, discussing your sexual-abuse issues with a skilled therapist will empower you.

In general, suggesting that one can just think their way out of such turmoil by ignoring its existence is consistent with the minimizing and denial, errors in thinking, often engaged in by the client. Of course, every victim of abuse, in their first efforts to resolve the abuse, attempts to minimize its impact ("It's not that bad—I will just stop thinking about it, and it will go away"). I am disappointed to hear this approach offered as a legitimate therapeutic technique. Minimizing and denying the power of the fear, anxiety, and frustration within will not resolve the aftermath of significant traumatic events such as sexual abuse.

For those individuals who have suffered both forms of damage, parental abandonment and sexual abuse, the effects, at the least, are additive. These powerful Icons that represent parental abandonment and sexual abuse send out Iconic echoes that reinforce and support each other. Like two earthquakes on separate shorelines that trigger waves to flow across the ocean, rogue waves form when the waves of one earthquake meets the other. The voices within become louder and more pervasive, especially when the primary statement of the first Icon, "You deserved what happened to you," finds repetition and reinforcement from the second, forcing the obvious conclusion: "You are not worthy of nurturing parents or having your body and your sexual essence treated with respect." This type of inner voice may take on a power that will force a psychotic resonance: "Everyone knows I'm bad," and eventually an obsession with addictions that will redirect thoughts and energies to any distraction that brings a miniscule amount of comfort and a moment of relief.

In summary, both parental abandonment and sexual abuse have the potential to be amongst the most damaging events an individual can experience. The aftermath of either is often years of self-condemnation and shame, which tend to be addressed with self-medication and the development of a vulnerability to some form of addiction. However, when the problem is conceptualized in terms of survival strategies required at the time of the abuse, strategies which are no longer necessary after the abuse has ended, then thoughts of change can be considered. When the ugliness within is conceptualized as a negative Icon still emanating condemning thoughts and feelings, then plans to shut down the Icon can be made. Once energy is removed from the negative Icons within, then the here-and-now problems of the present can be more easily addressed and resolved.

For those of you who have endured these difficult and potentially soul-destroying experiences, now is the time to understand what is happening within your mind: to understand the Iconic source that shapes the ebb and flow of your thoughts and feelings. You can then prepare your own road map and discern your own direction out of the confusion within. That is your healing journey. If you have already begun by sharing your secret abuse, injustice, and personal suffering, please know and accept that the sharing is just the beginning. The acknowledgement to a trusted witness is very important, but it is only the first step. There are more steps for you to take. Let us set that aside for now and consider how other very negative experiences often faced in adulthood are theoretically similar to the traumatic impact of parental abandonment and sexual abuse.

CHAPTER 8
Coping with and Overcoming Icons That Form in Adulthood

Surviving Death Experiences

After parental abandonment and sexual abuse, there is a third Icon, which generally forms later in life. This is the Icon that results from near-death and death-related experiences. Even those of you who have had a relatively wholesome upbringing can be struck down psychologically by the sudden and tragic death of a loved one. His or her death may bring about extreme levels of anxiety and disturbing nightmares that are overwhelming. When you tragically lose a son or daughter, brother or sister, mother or father, as a consequence of a murder, suicide or accidental death, the aftermath can be devastating. The Iconic echo that begins ("Life is terribly unfair; there is no justice; life is filled with danger") may never leave you. Often, those who suffer these types of trauma do not attend therapy, as they believe their wounds are too tender for discussion. On the positive side, when the time is right, many have the verbal skills to put words to the tragedy that they have experienced. They often find their own way, without assistance, to slowly come to terms with the tragedy in their lives.

▶ Death of a loved one

With those suffering from death-related experiences that involve the loss of a loved one, meeting with a psychologist or health-care professional will usually speed the healing process. Often however, those who suffer these tragedies do not want a speedy recovery. They would rather linger psychologically near the tragedy as a means of keeping close to the deceased and holding that person's spirit-presence within their own personality.

I have helped numerous clients who were dealing with the aftermath of murder or suicide in their family of origin. One woman, when she was eight years old, witnessed her mother murder her father. For over 20 years, she had not been able to escape the horrible images emanating from the memory of that experience. Another client had endured the suicide deaths of three family members.

For those of you who have suffered these types of tragedies, the disclosure and discussion of the memory is the important first step. I encourage you to find the strength to discuss what occurred with a therapist or psychologist. Often, the discussion is enough to bring relief and a return to the responsibilities of everyday life. However, for many, more than discussion will be required. Taking part in a role play with the deceased person will allow deep healing to occur.

I understand that when you suffer the loss of a loved one you will experience and live within extreme emotional pain, pain that may leave you temporarily only to return later with great intensity. A role play will bring that pain to the forefront of consciousness, where it can be addressed, softened, and released. I realize that considering this type of therapeutic intervention may appear almost beyond comprehension. For true healing to occur, however, you will come to understand that this type of role play is very helpful.

The first woman cited above, the woman who had witnessed her mother murder her father, was able, with great difficulty, to complete the role play with the therapist playing the part of her mother. She was able to ask her mother why she had murdered her father. She was able to express her long-repressed anger and disappointment. Finally, she was able to find forgiveness for the mother. Later, she was also able to come to terms with her deceased father by completing the "goodbye" role play with the Icon representing his memory, even though her feelings of loss and sadness for her father were of lower intensity than her anger and frustration for her mother.

The second lady, who had endured the suicide of three family members, completed role plays with each lost loved one, expressing not only her sadness and love but also her anger and disappointment.

Prior to these therapeutic interventions, both of these women had for years soothed their pain with alcohol and drugs. Their memories were powerful and would invade their thoughts on a daily basis. Both of these women were at times impulsively angry and aggressive. When triggered, their anger and aggression were beyond their control, and they would violently assault others. Both reported a tremendous sense of release following the disclosure and role-play exercises. After their courageous efforts in the treatment program, they became women much better prepared to return to their responsibilities. Both were ready to return to their role of nurturing mother for their children.

If you have suffered the loss of a loved one and remain continually reminded of that loss, then you should consider addressing these concerns. In individual counselling, where the Iconic approach is used, you would begin by discussing in detail the loss of your loved one, how it happened, how you reacted, how you continue to experience that loss and how you believe your present means of coping are no longer helpful. After this disclosure you will feel somewhat relieved but still you may carry tremendous sadness and grief. A role play with the lost loved one is the next exercise in the Iconic approach.

Your lost loved one, played by the therapist, might begin the role play by saying something like this:

> They have let me come back to have one last talk with you. What is it that you wanted to say to me?

Then it would be your turn to speak, to say what needs to be said. You might want to say this:

> It's just not fair that you died. It wasn't your fault—you did nothing to deserve that. I feel guilty that somehow I am still here and you're not. I will never be happy without you being here. I loved you so much, and now you are gone.

The lost loved one might say the following:

> I loved you too, but now I am gone. I don't want you to grieve my death forever. I want you to live your life fully, for me, if that is helpful. I don't want you to be continually distracted by my sudden and unfair death. For sure, grieve for a while. Then let me go and take on your journey in life to live it as best you can.

Sharing these feelings in the role play, feelings that are so difficult to express, will bring healing. When you think about it, it is very difficult to find a situation where these thoughts and feelings can be shared with an understanding person who is able to listen and respond. When these words are spoken in the role play situation, the feelings held since that horrible day find release, and finally you will find that you are beginning to move forward.

In our journeys in life, people we love die. Sometimes they die before they should. It is a tragedy. It is part of our journey to endure the pain and suffering. It is also our responsibility, when the time is right, to move forward, to move beyond that pain, to be able to give fully our love and support to those who remain, for those who depend upon us.

▶ Death of a comrade

Another type of death experience, which is often underestimated, is that suffered by soldiers in combat. If you are one of our brave soldiers who witnessed the death of a comrade, you may have been devastated not only by the loss of a friend but also by the aftermath; the recurring memory or flashback that continues to visit you, often awakening you from sleep. As well, the first responders in our community—our police officers, crime-scene investigators, and paramedics—witness horrific acts of violence and devastation at crime scenes and traffic accidents. Over the years, they are continually exposed to these scenes of death and tragedy. Their frontline work may engender elevated levels of anxiety and a sense of survivor guilt that begins to build in the background of consciousness to a near-intolerable level.

Many of our protectors—the men and women who have kept us safe, our police officers, soldiers and paramedics—are suffering. As a community we need to be mindful that their efforts come at a great psychological cost. Thank you for your service to our country and our community, for your efforts to keep the world a safer place, for being our protectors and rescuers. Now it is our turn to look after you. Your brave efforts have led to pain and suffering within that you do not deserve. Please understand that you can move forward and beyond the memories that haunt you. You know that the guilt you feel for the actions you could not have taken is irrational. Let the principles of this theory be applied to your problems. If you are working in one of these protector professions, you do not have to soothe the imagery of death and the accompanying anxiety with alcohol and drugs every evening. There is a way out—a way to find peace within.

Destructive Icons can develop from these types of experiences, and these can limit and weaken even the strongest and most stable personalities. Treatment with the principles of Iconic therapy can be very effective. I have successfully used this approach with soldiers and police officers. Some of them suffered recurring nightmares. When these nightmares were connected to a traumatic event they had investigated, and then a role play was completed, the nightmares stopped.

Painful Emotional Experiences

▶ The loss of love, and healing for the broken-hearted

Young men and women can have painful emotional experiences that slow their development for two or three years, or longer. Many have suffered the sadness and pain of lost love. The betrayal by a boyfriend or girlfriend and the sadness that follows can often devastate a sensitive and caring young person. This too can be handled using the Iconic principles. Often the longing for the lost loved one who will never return is mentally reviewed on a daily basis for years, generally during moments of loneliness. The Iconic reactions of "I was not good enough," "I am unlovable," or "I will never find love again" can reverberate and serve as the foundation for depression and a lackluster effort in the tasks of daily life.

If you are suffering this type of painful history and cannot seem to get over the lost precious love, then find a therapist and disclose how you feel. Then take on the "goodbye role play," a role play where you admit your love and longing for the lost romance. Take control of the painful memories and say to your lost lover what should have been said. Tell him or her that this conversation will be the last; you are saying goodbye; you are moving forward again. Say those words that you never spoke. This will release you.

> I just want you to know that I loved you and that love remains within me. I want to thank you for the beautiful memories that remain. I cherish those memories, in a way, too much. Now, I am saying goodbye from deep within me. It is time for me to move forward.

If you are still hanging on to past love, you know that it prevents you from giving all of your love to your next (or present) partner. You know, deep within your heart, that you want to be a man or woman who is capable of making the full commitment in the relationship with the partner you finally choose. Rise to that level by leaving the past behind and loving completely in the promises and commitments you give to your next lover. Do not be so wounded from past embraces that you enter into the next relationship unable to give what should be given. What will result is another broken heart: the heart of someone who deserves much more than that. Rise to the level of your potential—that of a person who, when the time is right, can love completely with their partner and then with their children.

▶ The shattering consequences of domestic violence

Another Icon that develops during adulthood is that brought on by violence within a loving relationship. Many of the women I worked with in prison had endured the cyclical nature of domestic violence. They described powerful love relationships that would deteriorate into razor-edge tension and then erupt into violence, often perpetrated mutually, with the woman getting by far the worst of it. Many of the women I spoke with would casually mention that, yes, their common-law partner had struck them, but not that often, and for them, it was not that bad. As they became more honest, I learned that they had suffered broken bones, often ribs or facial bones. Some had been choked into unconsciousness. Many had lost teeth. Some had become slaves to their partners in their efforts to sooth the raging beast that might emerge. Even with this horrible history, you could see optimism and hope in their hearts: the hope that somehow it would never happen again, that he would see the light, that the AA program he was attending was the answer. These ladies were deaf to the advice of their friends. They refused to hear the logic offered: that they were being destroyed in a cycle of abuse that was spiraling to a more and more violent conclusion. It was clear that they would be blindly returning to a hell that seemed beyond comprehension. These ladies needed to use the role play vehicle, often more than once, to find their voice, to demand their freedom, and to establish boundaries that could never be violated. When they took part in the role play, I would plant the seeds of truth in a gentle way by playing the part of the partner as impulsively abusive but repentant.

As the abusive husband, I would explain the power of the love that still existed for both:

> Kathy, you know I love you and want you back. It was just your mom and your friends who talked you into leaving me. You are my kindred spirit—we belong together. I promise I will never hurt you again. Can you forgive me? I will go to the counselling. I will do anything to prove my love for you.

I would hint at future violence by denying responsibility for the past:

> Kathy, you know it wasn't all my fault. Sometimes, you provoked me. That's not right either. You know when I'm upset you shouldn't bother me. You know

that. If you could work on that part, then I wouldn't
be so violent.

I would set the stage for the renewal of the destructive
relationship, while at the same time encouraging her to resist, to
take control, to be a woman who could say no to future abuse:

Kathy, I hear you. I know you think it's over. You're
right. Can't we just be friends? Can we meet for coffee?
Can I phone you now and then? Let me drive you to
work. What would be wrong with that?

If you are a woman involved in a relationship that becomes
violent, the Iconic principles of this therapeutic approach will help
you see the truth about how you are living. You do not have to
sacrifice your dignity and your body to violence in order to have love
in your life. There is a way out. If you can complete the role play
and be strong, then you can win back your freedom. Your freedom
will not be handed back to you. You have to be able to fight for it.
You will need to find your voice to say no to violence. I have heard
battered women say the following in the role play:

Our relationship is over. We can't be friends. It
would be too hard. You hurt me; you hit me. That's
unacceptable. You violated my trust in you. You took
advantage of the love I gave. Now I can never trust you
again. One angry look from you, and I will think of
all the times you hit me. I don't want to live like that.
Please stay out of my life.

These are tough words to say, but this is the sentiment that needs
to be communicated. Of course, there is a caveat with domestic
violence concerns. I am not encouraging anyone to directly confront
a person known to be violent when they, the victim, would be

vulnerable to being hurt again. Some of the women I worked with were partners with very dangerous men, such as those found in biker gangs. To extricate from these relationships is not easy. That is why the role play is completed in a safe environment, as it allows the participants to find their voices. It allows them to establish within themselves a concept of personal strength and a philosophy of independence and integrity in the presence of those who will offer support and encouragement. With this new-found strength and philosophy, they will find themselves in a better position to separate from the violent relationship.

Negative Environmental Stressors

There is another Icon-like negative energy emitter that is often seen in the offices of psychologists. This phenomenon is a function of negative environmental stressors or cultural dispositions and prejudices placed upon the developing personality in the form of the message "You're not good enough to make it." It is a function, in part, of the inability of the personality to cope with the ongoing negative stressors of the environment. These negative energy forces do not have the specificity that would allow for the creation of a negative Icon; rather, they are characterized by what I call a *resonator*: an energy force without a face that sends out negative energy to the personality. It competes with the positive Icons and positive Iconic echoes "You are loved and appreciated," and the conflict often causes the person to strive for perfection as a means of coping and fitting in. When perfection cannot be obtained, anxiety and depression often result.

There is a striving within the human condition for fairness. Democracies are founded, in part, on this basic principle: fairness for all. This is a high ideal and certain segments in the community often fall short. When individuals are treated unfairly, they are prone to develop an inner resonator that spins out the message: "You are not good enough to be treated fairly, to be treated as an equal."

Often, antiquated forms of class conflict remain within a democratic society, and conventional forms of unfairness emerge. For example, "You are not from the right kind of family; therefore, you don't belong in the higher class; you don't deserve to be heard." Racism, in subtle and not-so-subtle forms, still exists. A disguised message, "Your opinion is weak," is often merely a manifestation of "Your skin color is not quite right." Bullying is another example of extreme unfairness: "You're weak/different, so we will hurt you." Sexual-orientation stereotyping is another form of unfairness that our gay citizens endure: "God won't love you because you're gay."

This type of unfairness occurs in any situation where an individual in a position of power takes advantage of that power so that the rights and freedoms of others are compromised. The Iconic echo is "You're not good enough," and the Iconic reaction is one of general inadequacy: "I'll pretend I don't care about finding my potential, because there is too much risk for humiliation from important others if I fail." This is not a trauma-based resonator, but rather a resonator developed primarily as a result of ongoing negative conditioning within the general environment. These issues can be dealt with in Iconic therapy.

In general, we have to acknowledge that life's journey is often difficult. Unfair and unjust circumstances that visit us can be painful and powerful enough to destroy us. Cherished loved ones die. People commit suicide. Comrades are killed. Love relationships deteriorate to violence. We face unfairness in dealing with the unjust aspects of our community.

We often feel alone, lost, and overwhelmed with tragedy and unfairness, but an enduring, beautiful, and unique life force remains within. It is up to us to release it. It is for us to face the Icons of lost loved ones and have that final conversation in role play, to communicate our love and loss. It is up to us to face the unfairness that will visit all of us in some fashion. In this effort, from this vortex of confronted unfairness, our true selves will be released—the selves who will not tolerate abuse.

> *I'm 28 years old … I was once a scared victim. I suffered several years of abuse in different forms. My father was physically and mentally abusive. Due to this abuse and my lack of understanding, I learned to be a victim. My lack of emotional growth made me a perfect victim without a voice. I ran into teenage predators. I was eight years old when a sixteen-year-old exposed himself to me. I was a perfect victim. I never told.*

> *Next was far worse. It was a rape. I was 12 years old. Once again, I never told. The truth is, I never thought I deserved to be heard. I was a shy, angry girl who had low self-esteem. I continued to abuse myself with drugs to try to help me cope. In turn, I destroyed my life and hurt everyone I loved.*

> *I abused drugs for 17 years. Although the forms of substances changed, the consequences didn't. For the last seven years, I've found myself in and out of prisons. This time, I arrived a broken victim full of despair. Through the grace of God and a program called Courage of Women I found the courage to talk.*

> *I shared my pain, trauma, and abuse with women who were like me. I and so many women were broken, and our solution was drugs. I wasn't alone. I did not deserve to feel sad, scared, ashamed, or unimportant any longer. I developed a very different perception of myself and the women like myself.*

We did not deserve to be abused. Someone does care. We don't have to carry that shame and guilt any longer. We no longer have to be a scared victim without a voice. I then found my voice. I will no longer be a victim without a voice. I want to let others know that they are not alone. They don't deserve to be abused. Nobody does. They don't have to hurt themselves because some perpetrators made them feel like they deserved it. They too can find their voice! They too can stop being a victim without a voice and become a survivor with a story.

CHAPTER 9
Seven Basic Principles for Change

At this point, for clarity, the theoretical foundation and the basic principles learned during the development of Iconic therapy may help you understand what is required to successfully heal from past trauma, abuse, and unfairness.

Overarching Theoretical Foundation

The formation of the personality around negative Icons is a naturally occurring survival-driven phenomenon that is universal. It affects all of us. The aftermath of trauma (or a troubling negative experience) results in the formation of a negative Icon. Its impact is in proportion to the perceived risk to one's life or one's integrity. Its initial purpose is to protect the developing personality from similar future threats. However, it takes on a counterproductive nature once the individual has left the situation or circumstances that are of high threat. For some, the counterproductive nature of the Icon is worse than for others. The presence of a negative Icon establishes, at a minimum, a higher level of vigilance, guardedness and anxiety. In general, in proportion to the initial threat (or series of threats) one's focus narrows to primarily survival strategies and their perception of reality is skewed accordingly. This leads to a mindset where, more often than reality would dictate, a situation will be perceived as potentially threatening or harmful, when it is not.

This theory and its refinement, as noted earlier, were developed by working with those incarcerated individuals whose histories revealed significant dysfunction. Their experiences of the extremes of parental abandonment, sexual and physical abuse, and exposure to the death of loved ones allowed for the development of basic principles regarding the nature of the personality, how it forms under duress and, more importantly, how it can be changed. It is hypothesized that these same principles hold even for those with personal problems that are of a more minor nature. These principles apply to all of us.

▶ Principle 1: You cannot do it alone. A healing (therapeutic) relationship is required.

The first basic principle in Iconic therapy is that you cannot do it alone. You cannot heal yourself by yourself. A trusted person who has a healthy view of reality, or a group of individuals who together can communicate a realistic concept of fairness and justice in relation to your circumstance, is required to hear you share the unfair events that you have endured.

Reading about your problems and reading about solutions are good first steps, but a healing relationship is required for you to move forward. Reading and discussing problems like yours will be helpful. It may allow you to realize at an abstract level that what happened to you was not your fault; it was caused by the problems of others. You will find comfort with that solution, but deeper healing requires the emotional release that begins when you share the truth (in some detail) with another trusting person. As well, and more importantly, when the time is right, another person is required, to speak (in a role play) for the Icon so that your stored emotions can be released. It is essential to find a psychologist or an understanding counsellor with whom to share your history of abuse, so that you can heal.

▶ Principle 2: You need to acknowledge the depth of your problem.

The second principle or requirement for success in Iconic therapy is the acknowledgement of the deeper problem. Many of you will not realize the pervasive and insidious omnipresence of your core problem(s). You may, for example, describe your problem as depression. This generally is not your core problem but rather a symptom or manifestation of a deeper issue. In essence, in Iconic terms, the problem often has been a traumatic or life-threatening/altering experience never dealt with, such as abandonment or abuse from mother and/or father, sexual abuse, or the death of a cherished family member or friend. Many of you will secretly pretend that the core problem has been dealt with, or you will adopt the belief that it has faded away. With the interviewing and probing from a skilled psychologist or counsellor, the true nature of your core problem(s) can be revealed. At a minimum, you need to understand that, for healing to occur, the core problems need to be addressed.

▶ Principle 3: You must let go of your guardedness, your secrecy, and your shame.

When you have a core problem, an Icon forms and defensive reactions are developed to protect your true self. These defensive reactions include guardedness, secrecy, and shame. Initially these feelings kept you safer in the abusive environment where you endured trauma and unfairness. Now your defensiveness (guardedness) prevents healing and has to be set aside. This means that for survival purposes many of you will have minimized the impact of the core problem as a means of coping. (This is often one of the first strategies for survival.) This strategy continues into the present. In fact, as a continuation of this strategy, you might even deny that the problem still remains or you may believe the problem remains but that it cannot be changed—so why bother acknowledging its presence. Pretending that your core problem is not a problem is an error in thinking that supports keeping secret what happened to you. Generally, your survival strategies will have desensitized you to the power of the problem that you have endured for years and, with this effort, you will have convinced yourself that it no longer exists or that its presence is of little importance.

In spite of your efforts at conceptualizing your inner problems as solved or forgotten, you will also realize that there is something wrong with the life you are living. This may lead you to reading books of this nature and, when you are brave enough, your defensive strategies will soften and you may come to understand that those earlier core problems did have a significantly negative impact on your life. Most of you will consider attending a counsellor and, when you do, you will eventually admit that you were traumatized when you were younger. For example, when asked, you may be able to acknowledge that you were treated unfairly by parents or sexually abused by a babysitter. However, you may refuse to acknowledge that the past traumatic experiences remain a problem. This may be a defensive maneuver on your part to maintain well-practiced but unproductive survival strategies that keep you safe by keeping you quiet regarding the suffering you have endured. As a consequence you have a strong urge to not reveal the images and thoughts of the traumatic experiences that have altered your life and a concomitant urge to minimize the damage done.

It will be very difficult to concede that a traumatic memory is still tender and painful, and you will continue to say to yourself what you hope is true: "The sexual abuse doesn't bother me anymore," or "I don't care that my parents abandoned me," or "I will never risk loving; love is for fools." Your defensive strategies especially that of denial, may have been so successful that you are not aware at a conscious level the nature of the pain that remains. These defensive strategies and their accompanying viewpoints protect you from acknowledging the terrible sense of loss and/or shame that you hold. These same strategies prevent you from addressing these issues in situations where you are safe and where you could take action.

Your inaction is easily and often triggered by the negative Iconic echo within that resonates with, "Somehow, you are not worthy."

It is consistent with your deeply engrained survival strategies that you avoid addressing the deep problems within. You will experience a strong inner resistance to taking part in the therapeutic exercises recommended, even though, from a logical perspective, they seem harmless. Here are typical examples of efforts to minimize and deny core problems that have prevented others, many just like you, from taking the steps required to become a fully functioning person who is able to live up to their potential.

> My parents never loved me. Deep down, I know that I am unlovable. It's pointless to try to change what cannot be changed. Besides, I am past that now.

> I was sexually abused when I was younger, but I have dealt with that. It no longer bothers me. It's in the past; I'm focused on the future. It has nothing to do with my drinking and my problems with intimacy.

> My husband has beaten me many times. I know he will stop. I love him so much. He says he will stop and I believe him.

> My son died. I will never get by it. I secretly believe it was my fault. My life will never be the same. I will go back in time to try and undo what has been done and then return to live inside despair.

> My boyfriend/girlfriend, the love of my life, my perfect soul mate, left me. I was, and remain, shattered. I will never love again.

For those of you who suggest that you have dealt with your historical problems by secretly clinging to the rationalizations noted above, or similar cognitive distortions, you will be encouraged to take part in the treatment strategies anyway, to allow you to seek out what I believe is a deeper solution. Please understand that your guardedness, your resistance, and your shame are strategies that protected you before, but they now prevent your healing. Be strong enough to overcome your resistance, and face your deeper issues. Fight against your rationalizations with the inner thought "I am going to try these strategies—the risk of embarrassment and humiliation is worth the potential reward of healing."

▶ Principle 4: The Icon must be confronted in role play.

In Iconic therapy, it is necessary to confront the source of the core problem in role play. This allows for the emotional release of feelings previously repressed for survival purposes. The role play generally leads to a healing catharsis. Merely talking about or disclosing the trauma will not allow the emotional release in its complete form and full healing will not occur.

When an Icon is confronted in role play, a traumatic memory is addressed. When the role play is completed successfully, which occurs when the residual emotions from that difficult event are expressed, the memory trace is permanently altered. Following the role play, the traumatic memory trace will have a new ending, and the repressed feelings previously attached to that memory trace will no longer be present with the same emotional reactivity. This new mental condition will allow for a sense of quiescence in the place where that memory trace was stored.

I believe that one session with a role play where the abuser is symbolically confronted is roughly equivalent to 20 sessions of speaking about the abusive experience. Who can afford 20 sessions of therapy? When clients continue to return and just speak about the abuse, they generally become weary from the effort and begin to believe that they are not making enough progress—and at an emotional level, they may not be. They secretly come to an understanding: "I will never be free of this negativity, this anxiety that holds me back." Eventually, they just stop talking about it. Usually, in conventional therapy, they are not asked to do the role play. Thus, they never experience the integrating power of directly expressing the deeply rooted toxic emotions that remain attached to the trauma.

In Iconic therapy the client is advised and encouraged by the therapist that the role play leads to freedom from the emotional power of the Icon, and to an eventual elimination of the Iconic echo ("You're no good"). This exercise is very powerful. Many times, I have seen how it plays a major role in transforming extremely damaged clients from flight-oriented, timid victims to the fight-ready confident survivors who look forward to life's challenges rather than continually reflecting back to past trauma. This process has been proven in extreme cases. The principles for change also hold for the less extreme. One must come to understand that there is talking *about* the Icon and then there is talking *to* the Icon. Remember, the healing journey is difficult. Prepare yourself for battle. Summon your courage. Muster your resources. Call on your strength. You can take on the Icon directly and change your mental life.

▶ Principle 5: Symbolic acts will allow you to break free of the Iconic echo and the attached errors in thinking.

The irrational hold of the Iconic echo can be addressed through symbolic efforts, as the Icon itself is merely a symbol of a traumatic memory trace. These symbolic acts soften the echo and will free the client to set aside, at a deeper level, the errors in thinking and especially lingering errors in feeling ("I feel shame for being part of that abuse") that have inundated their emotional life.

In Iconic therapy, there is one symbolic act, the "Cloak of Shame" (which will be discussed in a later chapter), that gently launches healing energies and attitudes towards the negative Iconic symbols that are stored from past trauma. This exercise addresses directly, but in symbolic form, the shame that generally attaches to the memory of abuse. The client is reminded of what they already know, namely, that they did not deserve to have been subjected to abandonment, abuse, unfairness and disrespect. In addition they are reminded that it is no longer necessary to carry the shame attached to those unsettling experiences. Talking about setting aside the shame is helpful, but the shame remains. The act of putting on a cloak that represents the shame, acknowledging that one carries shame that is not theirs, and then casting the cloak off, symbolically releases the shame.

This exercise is based upon the principle that memories are stored and organized as symbols. Shame, however, is a feeling, attached to a memory. It has not achieved a symbolic form. Once it is identified as having an existence, once it is presented as a burden that weighs upon you, then it begins to take on a symbolic form. Then it can be understood as something that can be removed. The Cloak of Shame exercise fulfills that function.

▶ **Principle 6: When the Icon is successfully confronted, defensive structures well established within the psyche fall away, and the inner spirit is freed to leave the past behind, to live more in the present, and to prepare to move forward.**

I first noticed this "falling away" concept when I helped clients with their upsetting dreams. Often, a client would attend the group and would be reluctant to take part. However, he or she would come to me as the group was ending, in those closing moments when it was too late to spend the time required for anything but the exit. The client would present a difficult problem, in this example, an upsetting dream, and a competing counterproductive attitude: "I need your help, but now there is no time, so I tried, but I lost again." At least the client felt comfortable enough in the therapy setting to take this calculated risk.

I would make the time for the person. She might tell me that she was having the same frightening dream every night, so frightening that often she would try to avoid going to sleep. One woman, who had been raped while sleeping, would dream the rape was about to re-occur when she did fall into sleep. In her dream a man was entering her room with the intention to hurt her. She would awaken terribly frightened, unable to return to sleep. I handled this situation, in the five minutes stretched for her benefit, by first explaining the basic premise that in our dreams, as in our lives, we have to face our fears. It is essential that we take control of our inner lives. It is important that our inner energy flows against evil and wrongdoing and that we do not cower within. I asked her to practice, with me, saying to the rapist in her dream who was entering her room: "Get the hell out of here! Get out of my room, and get out of my mind. You will never do that to me again!"

I would ask her to imagine saying this in her mind as if she could change the dream. She would then imagine speaking her part two or three times. Next, if she was strong enough, I would ask her to say it out loud to me as if I were that person coming into her room. She would try. Then, I would ask her to stand, take a position of assertiveness and strength, and say it. Last, I would ask her to tower over me, as I remained seated, and say the confrontational statements. Then, I would encourage her, as part of her preparation for sleep, to practice saying and imagining these confrontational themes and actions, just before settling to sleep. The results were generally excellent. Often the recurring dreams that had haunted her and clients like her for years stopped. At a minimum, their dreams would be altered to less-frightening ones. What was even more interesting than the successful outcome was their reaction. They began, almost immediately, to present as if they had never suffered the dreams, as if the experience of the bad dreams had been forgotten. I would ask at the next meeting about what had happened with the dream. The response would be one of acknowledgement: "It worked." But, rather than a big celebration, they would be immediately ready to move to their next concern, as if the last obstacle, the dream, had never been there or had not been as terrifying as first described.

I began to understand the traumatic dream as an old structure that had just fallen away into dust. It was as if it had disappeared and no longer existed, not even as a memory. From a therapeutic perspective, it was perfect. The trauma memory that had been so frightening was totally beaten—to the point that it was no longer there. Even the memory of its existence was, for the most part, gone. What could be better than that? The old structures had disappeared, and energies for the journey forward were now enhanced, less vulnerable to fear and distraction, and more focused.

I have implemented this approach with numerous clients, and it always resulted in improvement. The dreams either stopped or become less threatening. I believe it is the ephemeral qualities of dreams that allow them to disappear, with the correct intervention and response. In a similar way, I believe the memories of the trauma itself, experienced consciously in those times of full awareness; will also fall away when the exercises of this program are completed. Icons live in dreams, as well, and I believe they are easier to take on and eliminate than the ones that live in past memories. The past-memory Icons are tougher, but they too can be deflated and de-energized to reduce and possibly eliminate the power of their presence within the personality.

▶ Principle 7: You must speak out against the injustice.

Full recovery from trauma is indicated when the victim speaks out in a public way in an effort to heal others and to bring healing to the community. When a person can speak against what occurred to him or her in a manner that addresses the pain and suffering of others who have been similarly traumatized, then healing finds its expression and affirmation in a concern for others. Therapeutic exercises that encourage the client to speak in a public format serve two purposes. The effort consolidates gains made at a personal level ("I found healing and you can too"). As well, this type of effort encourages action at a community level, where others are encouraged to redirect Iconic energy away from *flight* ("This kind of thing should be kept silent") and toward *fight* ("Let's all take action against this type of injustice; I want to warn and protect others"). This type of exercise addresses survival concerns in that other dimension: the dynamic within that supports our energies for the survival of our species. It fulfills our longing to help others like ourselves.

▶ The aggressive attitude required for success

These are the principles in Iconic therapy upon which the therapeutic strategies and interventions are based. If you take this healing journey, you will take risks and you will suffer anxiety, but—and this is the good part—you will move quickly to the heart of your problem. Please prepare yourself. This is aggressive therapy. Its purpose is to attack your problem, defined as the Icon within. It is your mission to take the power away from the Icon. You will end up with that power.

For the most part, your problems are a manifestation of the resonating Icons within, warning you of life-threatening danger, encouraging you to be afraid, and reminding you that your survival is being threatened, even when you are safe. Even if your problems seem minor in comparison with many described here, they instil within you anxiety, self-doubt, and self-hatred, that continue to interfere with your daily life. The strategies developed and explained below will work for you and will allow you to break free of that inner sense that something ominous and life-threatening is continually waiting for you.

Are you up for it? If you can read to the end of this book, part of you wants to do it. Your reading to this point tells me that you are considering the work required that will lead you to finding a greater sense of inner clarity and inner peace. You deserve to be in that place with that sense of at-oneness. I believe that you can find, establish and maintain this type of inner life.

Let us look at all the strategies developed in the prison program with women. They had suffered extreme abuse and, as a consequence, developed extreme, life-altering Iconic reactions that had allowed them to survive their abuse but diminished their potential for future growth. When I met with these courageous women, they were all drowning in their counterproductive survival strategies. They were lost in their undeserved shame and silence regarding past trauma.

The treatment exercises used in this program with people who had very overwhelming problems will work just as effectively with those of you whose problems are more minor. For your first exercise, let us go one step further. Let's pretend that the same type of group program is operating in the community and you (through the pages in this book) will be attending.

CHAPTER 10
What Would Happen If You Were to Attend an Iconic Workshop or Group-Therapy Program?

One of the most valuable things I've learned in life … in case any of you don't know yet, I'm proud to be the one to share it with you … a fact that has changed my life forever … The shame is not mine!

The Group Process

For the sake of your healing journey, try to imagine that you have finally made that decision to take part in an Iconic treatment program. A group program entitled "The Healing Journey" is available; one of your friends has been attending, and she has invited you.

When you attend the program, your first thought will be to pretend that you are okay, because in a way it is true; you are okay. You have survived the difficulties, the injustices, and the disappointments of your life so far. But you know there is more to life than what you have. You wish you could carry on without the anxiety and self-doubt that is always there. As well, you know that there is the hidden side to your personality. There are concerns that you have never really faced. These concerns weigh you down. For safety, you decide to begin the program with a cautious approach. If anyone asks, you will tell them you have just come to support your friend. You may admit to yourself that you have had problems, but to acknowledge them in front of a group of strangers would be taking too big a chance. Let's face it—you don't even know these people. Besides, you have been pretending that you are normal your entire life. It is as natural as the sun coming up in the morning for you—as it is for all of us, to minimize and deny the impact of our own personal issues. So, you will enter thinking, "I'm just an observer—I'll be okay just as I am."

Your inner voice (the *Iconic reaction*) will remind you that if you share what happened to you, you risk that all those present will conclude that somehow you deserved what happened. You have spent years convincing yourself that you should keep not only your past abuse or injustice secret but also the shame of it.

In the program, you will hear supporting and welcoming words from others. You will slowly be encouraged to believe that what happened to you happened to others as well. You will be surprised to learn that you are not alone! You will be encouraged to believe that the voice in your head that continually haunts you with negative thoughts about yourself, reminding you that you are less than others, is speaking lies and supporting tragic errors in thinking that are simply wrong-minded.

The psychologists or counsellors will remain patient when, at first, you decide to not fully acknowledge the extent of your problem. Those trying to help you must remember that when you live inside your head, it is difficult to gain a perspective regarding the far-reaching dimensions of the problem that lives there too. That problem impacts every life choice, especially the choice to deal with that problem.

Somehow, they know that you are apprehensive. In the first group, you are told by one of the other participants that, just like you, she was really nervous during her first meeting. She seems so confident. She speaks as an advocate for the group and tells you and the other newcomers that there are seven exercises or strategies required to complete the program—strategies that will lead to personal growth and a sense of freedom. You learn that one of the exercises is to serve as the advocate for the group and introduce new members. That is what this very encouraging lady is doing. You learn almost immediately that the first exercise, or requirement, is disclosure.

You are relieved to hear that, as this is your first time, you do not have to talk or share anything. You can just observe. This allows you to breathe a little easier. In fact, you learn that you can choose to *never* speak about what happened to you. However, you also come to know that the group leader and the others will be encouraging you to take the first step on what they call "the healing journey," as they truly believe it will be a helpful thing for you to do. Putting all that aside, you relax as best you can and just sit and listen.

Almost immediately, you realize that most of the others are volunteering to take the next step in their journey. You observe another group member sharing her story for the first time. You observe the person disclosing, crying in the effort, and this is accepted by the therapist and by the others. Many in the group offer supporting remarks. You realize that you are touched by the deep level of honesty, courage, and sharing. As your problem is very similar to that of the lady who is sharing, you feel tears welling in your eyes. You identify with her pain and suffering, because it is very similar to yours. When you are asked for your comments, after hearing the encouraging remarks of others, you are able to offer a supportive remark because your longing to be helpful is stronger than your urge to stay silent. In an effort to comfort the lady who disclosed, you spontaneously admit that, yes, you also were abused, but you have never spoken about it. Your fear is recognized, and your reluctance is respected: "You don't have to disclose today—or any day, for that matter—only when you are ready."

You begin to take on a new perspective. Maybe disclosing is something you *can* do. Maybe your childhood survival strategy for secrecy is no longer required. Maybe telling your story is something you could manage, as the others have survived sharing their disclosures and seem somehow happy with their efforts, not destroyed. An analogy is shared by the group leader with another woman who is attending for the second time. It is obvious that she is very afraid to speak. She is told the following:

> It's as if you are going to a train station. Everyone is getting on the train to freedom. You think, as it leaves the station, "I don't belong on that train." Then, all of a sudden, you are on it. You can feel yourself moving forward for the first time since it happened. It is a good feeling.

You think that maybe you will get on that train.

Revealing the Core Problem

You may be one of those individuals who, when asked about the nature of your primary problem, will respond with, "It is drugs and alcohol; I want to stop but I can't." You will be gently encouraged to understand that this may not be your primary problem but rather the primary solution to your deeper core problem.

Eventually, you will come to accept that your psychologist or counsellor has methods to help you break free of whatever it is that has such a hold on you. He or she understands and accepts your reticence and reluctance. Somehow, he[8] knows that your personal history contains unresolved pain and suffering that you have survived and are trying to forget. You will always be given permission to keep your secrets, to hold and maintain your very private (although most

---

[8] The therapist can be a man or woman and for the sake of simplicity, in this chapter, the therapist will be presumed to be a male.

likely distorted) view of your personal history. He will understand if you minimize and deny the problems of your past, as this type of perception has been important for your survival thus far.

As well, please know and trust that your therapist or counsellor will listen to your denial and minimization. He will not dismiss or discount what you say in a coercive manner, as this type of approach itself is abusive and disrespectful and has no legitimate place within the dialogue between client and counsellor. However, your therapist will ask you to be honest about what happened to you. You may be making efforts to minimize your problem, presuming that, even though something did happen, it was not that bad; or, even if it was bad, it is now practically forgotten; or, if it is not forgotten, at least it is no longer as painful as before. So, even though you are using all of these descriptors to allow yourself some sense of protection, you will still be encouraged to say whatever it is that you have to say. You need to disclose the truth about your history, saying whatever it is that applies to you:

I was sexually abused by …

My parents were alcoholics and neglected me.

I was given up for adoption, and I began to believe I was unlovable.

My son committed suicide, and I can't live with it. It was my fault.

My husband betrayed me and I can't forgive him.

My dad had such high expectations, I could never do anything right. I feel like a loser even when I'm not. I still love my dad but I can never please him.

A bad thing happened to me when I was a teenager,
and I'm ashamed.

Disclosing the traumatic experience in enough detail to allow
its release is essential for progress. The fear of further personality
disintegration, supported by a strong sense of shame and self-loathing,
are obstacles that prevent sharing. With disclosure, there is a sense of
integration, pride, and accomplishment. In my opinion it is a truly
personal victory. In Iconic language, when you disclose your deep
problem, the Icon is exposed, and its weaknesses become obvious.

The Icons that live in your mind are like vampires. When they
live in secrecy in the dark recesses of your mind they are powerful,
but when they are exposed to the light, when the truth of their
history is shared with others, they are weakened. They can then
be removed from their place of power. It is these Icons that have
been distorting your ability to comprehend and understand your
abusive experience. They have led you to distortions regarding your
self-worth and your integrity. These distortions support a sense of
shame and guilt; they have echoed (the Iconic echo) throughout
your personality and inhibited your efforts to move forward on
your personal journey. These Icons hold you back from your efforts
to discover your true self. They prevent you from actualizing the
essence of your being and inhibit your efforts at love. They limit
your longing for productive work that will benefit not only you but
also your family and community.

To say your core problem out loud to an understanding and
accepting witness (or witnesses) is the first step in taking control
of your inner life. It is the most important step. I encourage you to
take it.

▶ Changing Personal Strategies

In the initial stages of the Iconic program, you will generally need
to develop a personal belief that the therapeutic exercises that you

will be asked to complete will lead to healing or, at minimum, do no harm. As a person committed to your own healing, you will need to adopt the belief that you are strong enough to overcome your fears and anxieties regarding the exercises suggested for you. You may need time to develop this philosophy. You may need proof that it works. This proof will be obvious over time, as you watch the other participants begin to change. You will see them arrive at places of insight and self-acceptance. Then you will say to yourself, "I want that; I want to be there." Slowly, you will come to believe in the steps along the healing journey. Slowly, you will begin to feel embraced by the acceptance of the group, the therapeutic alliance that builds with each meeting. At the same time, the psychologist will be encouraging you to realize that your strategies ("don't share, don't trust"), which once were essential and survival-oriented, are now counterproductive. You will be encouraged to accept the principles of the program, namely, that speaking the horrible truth about the past is the first step in the healing journey. It is very important that you come to believe that this is the first step. When you truly believe, with gentle encouragement, you will begin your healing journey.

▶ The Courage to Begin Manifesto

At different times during the workshop—when there is a lull, when the moment feels right, or sometimes at the close of an emotional group—the participants will read together the "Courage to Begin Manifesto" (see below). It helps those attending to accept the basic philosophy of the program. Each of the steps in the program is referred to in the Manifesto. It serves to encourage those who are afraid and to embolden those who want to move forward. Repeat this mantra until it is your own.

The Courage to Begin Manifesto

I believe in the healing journey.

I believe I have the courage to begin—to speak the hidden truth about what happened to me.

I will turn to the abusers who live in my mind. I will confront them with the pain, anger, and sadness forced upon me. I will find justice.

I will cast off the shame that was never mine and experience the freedom that living in the truth brings.

With this freedom, I will break through the barriers that limit my spirit and my voice.

I will mold my life into something I am proud of.

I will advocate for my children, for my brothers and sisters, and for the community.

I will allow the beauty of my inner spirit to be revealed. My loving heart will open to the beauty of others, having left pain and suffering behind.

When my personhood is tested, I will be a person of courage. My voice will be heard.

If you are to break free from the Icons within and the shame that limits you, each of you needs time to trust that this therapeutic approach will work for you. It is always assumed that you will know when you will be ready to begin. Reading the manifesto aloud helps to build hope that you will be able to overcome your fears, like those participants described below. Eventually you will come to know that you too, can begin a healing journey.

▶ Certificates Recognizing Achievement

Another component of the group program that helps participants feel validated for their work is the presentation of certificates. In the prison program, for every exercise completed a certificate was awarded. These certificates were extremely beneficial as they provided a sense of accomplishment and resulted in a heightened sense of self-esteem. Their presentation, generally at the end of the group session, served as a public recognition of the participant's progress through the various steps. Each certificate had the participant's name, date, and the identifying feature of the recent accomplishment (e.g., "First Disclosure") superimposed over vibrant images with symbolic meanings (e.g., a woman in profile, facing the rising sun in a yoga pose). Some participants remarked that the pictures had a calming quality that they would look to when upset. Often, they would show them to their families and use them when speaking of their progress to others.

Now that we are into the program, or at least contemplating such a shift in our personal strategies, let us think about and consider the first step in the journey forward, the disclosure.

CHAPTER 11

Step One: Disclosure

Hello, my name is … and I would like to share a bit about my experiences, in hopes that you may be able to learn from them. I learned from a young age to allow others (it didn't matter who) to use my body for whatever they liked and whenever they wanted. I think it began with my dad; he started fondling me at an early age. He would rub my breasts—even put his mouth on them—as well as use his hands to play with my private parts between my legs. I remember having to put my hands on his private parts to touch him while he was busy rubbing and sticking his fingers inside of me. I also vaguely remember that I was scared, not understanding, really confused as this was my mommy's husband. Something was not right, but would I make things even worse, or would it be blamed on me, if I said something? Vaguely, I remember something about this girl who I remember was a little older than me—learning from her—it is normal to be used as little girls, kinda like our job, what can we do about it? Just do it. I also have this thought of this girl making me do things with her and this guy she may have lived with. I am thinking that he used us both, and she taught me how it went. Also, all of this exposure to sexual stuff at such a young age, as well as vague memories with my cousin … long, long, ago came to my mind too, as all four of us cousins often would be sleeping together. He would touch and feel my private parts and, again, making me feel his genitals. In both, I remember my dad and my cousin always whispering to me, "Does that feel good?" I can remember them asking me that when they were rubbing their bodies against mine. With my younger sister and cousin lying so close, I would try to be as quiet as possible so that I would not expose them to such a gross ordeal.

I began to run away from home, as often as I could and how ever I could. I did not like being at home. I felt uncomfortable and not safe. I began drinking and using marijuana with friends around age 14 or 15, and smoking, too. I do remember, though, in elementary school when I began drinking and running away, a very old man who'd let me crash, hide out at his apartment. All I had to do was whatever he wanted (I honestly don't remember exactly), but he was a gross old man who liked little girls. Eventually, I chose not to go there, after letting him give me alcohol to visit, get naked, and touch me. It was gross. As I became more and more into partying, I was introduced to older users/partiers. Once I was drugged, and while drinking, I woke up, in and out of consciousness to three older guys forcing themselves on me and raping me. I hurt and was told not to tell. I was threatened and very scared. I remember being tossed out of that house and walking down the middle of the street towards my friends in complete shock, hurting physically and feeling mad. What and who was I going to tell that wouldn't bring up my other past abuse issues? So, silent again and safer, I figured. I then found myself using guys as they used me, except I just wanted to remain drunk and/or high in order not to think, so do what you want with me as long as I would not come to reality—because if I did I would be off to someone else where I could achieve what I wanted. I no longer wanted to feel—I did not know how to feel—I hated to feel, so I put a complete stop to that. Over time, I became involved in hard drugs and was introduced to a whole new lifestyle—different and better, or so I thought. Forced into a way of life and had no choice of my circumstances. Naive and new to the scene, I learned quickly how things went, so I thought. Well things changed pretty quickly over five years of that. Continuing to be used—always and whenever—so I felt constantly abused in many ways throughout and in such a lifestyle. Mind you, my self-worth, self-esteem, pride, ego, and self-respect had long ago been lost or set aside. I learned at a young age I was an object, or at least that is how I felt.

I am a victim of sexual abuse. I want to tell you that your life does not have to go the way mine did. I have learned since then, what has happened to me has not and had never been my fault. I was an innocent child, just like many of you. Things that you have heard me tell you today are my examples. I want to be completely honest and share with you, as none of these things that have happened were right. They are wrong—very wrong—and whoever does these things are the ones who are wrong, and they can and should be punished severely. Any type of abuse is uncalled for, but sexual abuse towards an innocent, helpless child is the worst, most despicable crime there is.

The Iconic group-therapy program was held twice per week, with approximately 10 members in attendance with two therapists. It was held in a prison for female inmates. The program evolved over a period of time to having seven important steps required to heal and release the true self. As these women were in prison, it was presumed that they had significant problems that interfered with healthy growth and development.

It was discovered early on that all of these imprisoned women had been exposed to a combination of damaging experiences, including parental abandonment/neglect/mistreatment, sexual assault/abuse/innuendo, sudden death by murder/suicide of loved ones, and/or other very negative environmental stressors. Their exposure to these damaging, potentially soul-destroying events led to the instillation of very powerful negative mental imagery, with the accompanying negative feelings in the mindset of these women. Although these inner feelings were survival-oriented (they predicted dangers ahead), attached to their presence was a sense of doom and a negative aura emanating from the memory of the abusive events. This negative aura washed over their sense of personhood, causing them to hold attitudes of self-condemnation and feelings of shame.

Most of the women presumed that there was no way out of this mental state of self-condemnation. Their reflexive apprehensions about impending doom and the attached self-hatred, both of which had been used to survive their past, were now contributing to their failure in the present. For many, their upbringing and the negative events they had endured had forced them to set aside most thoughts of personal growth and development. Their only concern was survival, even though, deep down, they knew that life had more to offer. Many had not been able to fulfill those other basic strivings in life that included connecting in a meaningful and intimate way with a partner, having and nurturing children and taking part in valued work. These failings led to very strong and potentially long-lasting feelings of resentment, anger, disappointment, discouragement, and sadness regarding the course of their lives.

For you, the reader, it is important to understand that the mental representative of your original trauma and its aftermath, the negative aura, have continued to have an impact upon you. I have conceptualized this negative memory as an inner Icon. From a theoretical perspective, this Icon has the power to not only bring back the original trauma to consciousness but also to poison any efforts you make to take on challenges that distract or separate you from the survival strategies you have developed.

When you complete the exercises established in this program, you will find release from these continually resonating, fear-provoking thoughts and feelings emanating from the Icon within. You will achieve a new understanding, integration with, and then separation from your past. Finally, you will incorporate an improved way to blend cognitive and emotional processes when communicating with others, without triggering strong, overwhelming feelings initially connected to the past trauma(s).

The first important sign of success you will notice will be that you will finally be able to speak about your abusive experiences without crying and without being overwhelmed with feelings of shame, anger, frustration, sadness, and self-loathing. With the completion of these exercises, you will begin to understand and accept, as part of your history, the undeserved horrors you experienced. Then you will be able to move beyond these traumatic experiences. You will begin to realize that your locus of control is now at the center of your true self, not shared with a negative Icon and the traumatic memories from the past.

This program was initially designed for those who had been traumatized as a result of sexual abuse. Then the program was expanded, as it was discovered that the exercises will work for any type of abusive or traumatic experience.

Shame and Fear Rise to the Surface During Therapy of this Nature

Most of the participants believed that their traumatic past condemned them to ongoing feelings of disgust and disrespect from within and from others (if the others were to learn the truth). They were burdened with an undeserved, but powerful, self-condemning sense of shame. They were afraid that if they shared their secrets—the sexual abuse or the domestic violence or the parental abandonment or the loss of a cherished loved one—the disgust, disappointment and critical nature of others would rain down upon them, and their uniqueness would be judged as unacceptable. They were afraid to reveal, even to themselves, their deep, unspoken suspicion that they were totally unworthy of respect. They presumed that others would condemn them, just as they had condemned themselves.

When they attended their first group, they observed something quite unusual and mildly upsetting. Other group members were speaking openly about their traumatic experiences. The newcomers would observe how difficult and troubling it was to share the pain of the past. In spite of that, there was a sacred quality about what was happening. The newcomers saw that when others spoke about their traumatic experiences, there was a riveting sense of honesty and sincerity. There were tears that expressed not only pain and sadness but also truth and purity.

The novices soon learned that disclosure of the abusive experience or experiences was the first step in "the healing journey." As well, with the observation of others disclosing and doing even more difficult exercises, such as the role play, they came to understand that there were tangible steps along the healing journey that the others were able to manage. Here is what two participants wrote about that difficult first step, the disclosure:

> *I feel the hardest step was "Disclosure." I mean, nobody really wants to open up those old wounds to feel like you yourself had committed a crime. But once I had told my story, and I knew that I was heard and believed, I gained a little more courage and wanted to see what else could help me …*

> *In the beginning, I found it very hard to reveal the secrets I had kept for so long. My wounds were very deep. I thought*

they would never heal. I felt ashamed, even though I was a victim. I felt humiliated by someone known to me and my family. I felt a heavy burden from the oracle I carried for so long. I turned to drugs and alcohol as a means to survive and hide how I felt inside. There was no one to trust, no place to be safe to release my burden. I did not know that a place to heal and a journey of courage awaited me.

If you are like most who attend the program, you might come once or twice and not disclose. Your reluctance will be accepted, but you will be encouraged to acknowledge, at a minimum, that disclosing the truth about your past could be a positive, albeit difficult, experience. You will witness others disclosing their very troubled histories, and you will observe the powerful impact this has, not only for the disclosing person but also for the entire group. You, like the others in the group, will accept without question the honesty of the disclosure, which is often given with a gut-wrenching effort that somehow proves its validity. It is more than clear that what is being shared comes from the deepest and sincerest place in that person.

When it is your turn to disclose, when that moment arrives and you know that it is the right thing for you to do, you also will know that this is a place where you feel safe in saying what has to be said. As you feel accepted in the therapeutic alliance that permeates the atmosphere; you will know that you remain a respected member of the group, whether you disclose or not. You will know that the choice is yours. You will also have come to the belief that it will be a difficult, but beneficial, experience for you to disclose; that it will be a positive step on your healing journey. From observing others, you also will understand that the disclosure may bring tears. That will be okay as well, as you will have witnessed others crying. You will now understand and accept that disclosing is the new survival strategy and replaces the old "keep-the-secret" strategy. Then you will share, often for the first time, the horrible event or series of events that you have kept hidden away.

Many of you will share some aspect of your hidden pain that you have never spoken of before. Some of you will have disclosed partially during prior treatment, but you will have more to say in this program. You may have previously shared all of your troubled past with a psychologist or therapist and yet still feel trapped or shamed by it. Some of you will have shared your story as part of a police investigation. Some of you may have told your story to a school counsellor but then recanted and said it wasn't true. This may have been at the encouragement of a family member. Maybe it was your mother who said, "Tell them something else; the family will be ruined if you tell them that." So you changed your story and told them you made it all up. That's okay. You were young and vulnerable then and maybe that was the only way out. It happens often, and as therapists, we understand.

When you share your story, you will discover what I have observed when someone shares. The sharing of the abuse is for the most part, a positive experience. As noted earlier, there has been a great deal of discussion amongst psychologists regarding the risk of re-traumatization. The fear is that you, the victim of abuse, will be transported back to the scene of the terrible event and be traumatized again, as if it is happening for the first time. This has never occurred in this program, most likely because all disclosures have been voluntary. Yes, the disclosure generally brings with it a great deal of emotion in the form of tears, frustration, shame and anger. These emotions however, should not be considered a return to the scene of the trauma but rather an effort to verbally and emotionally process what occurred. One has to remember that victims of abuse have thought about their abuse many times without sharing what occurred, yet wanting to somehow speak about, externalize and release the maelstrom of unexpressed thoughts and feelings that remain. Finally, with their disclosure, they can go beyond merely thinking about the injustice they have endured. Speaking the disclosure out loud to a trusted person or persons is not the shock to the system that many would suggest. It has been rehearsed mentally many times.

The Fight-or-Flight Scenario

The basic choice in most frightening situations is "fight or flight," to either run from the perpetrator or turn towards him and fight. With children and their generally vulnerable state, the choice has usually been a type of flight from the situation. The inner mindset forms as follows:

> Flee from the horrible event or horrible person; hide as best you can when he is around. Do not confront the abusive person in any manner—he is too dangerous. Do not let him feel guilty. That will make it worse for you. Keep what happened a secret. If it helps, flee from the truth as well. Do not examine the truth in any detail—it is too upsetting.

As a victim of abuse, even when you are older, you most likely will conduct yourself as you always have. You will continue to flee similar situations of threat. Some of you will try to take flight even from the truth and pretend it did not happen. When you arrive for treatment by way of the Iconic approach, you will be encouraged to shift the strategy from flight to fight, to confront the situation in symbolic form, first, by disclosing (confronting the secrecy), and second, in the role play (confronting symbolically the perpetrator).

When you first attend a group program or individual counselling, as noted above, you are advised of this therapeutic philosophy. It is new for you and represents a movement in another, more frightening, direction—towards the perpetrator or negative event. The thought of fighting or confronting this inner demon has never, or rarely, occurred to you. It was not an option if the negative event occurred when you were little and you programmed yourself to flee the situation in order to survive. That is why this approach is very difficult. It requires a significant change in strategy. However, if you are in "flight" modality, it is wrong to force you to change direction and strategy and insist instead that you turn and fight. If you are forced, as mentioned above, then it is quite possible that you will be re-traumatized. Because you are struggling for control of your inner psyche, your true self, the choice has to be yours.

First, you have to prepare yourself mentally for the shift of strategies. You can do this, by understanding the principles of Iconic therapy and by observing how others disclose the nature of their traumatic experiences. You need to believe that changing strategies has a good chance of success and a low chance of further damage being done. You need to sincerely accept that it is now time to turn around, to look evil directly in the eye, and fight for freedom—to take the chance, no matter how difficult.

The disclosing experience is not easy, and most of you will struggle with it. You will know from observing others that when you begin your disclosure it may be difficult. Always remember, you have survived the abuse. You are a survivor, and your words are now required to define and clarify what occurred to you. Tell your story and acknowledge the emotions that you could not share at the time of that horrible event, the emotions that could not safely find expression and release. Share your sadness, disgust, and anger for being sexually, physically, and/or emotionally assaulted. Share your deep sadness for losing what was lost. Speak about having your personal development slowed and your essence for life diminished. Release the voice that has been silenced for so long, your voice. Hear yourself speak the words that define and explain your pain and loss.

Remember, these pent-up feelings (e.g., anger, disgust, self-loathing, sadness) are often triggered by the Iconic echo during your everyday functioning. They have leaked into many aspects of your life and have poisoned your efforts to become the person you want to be. They caution you against striving for your true potential and warn of risks that are not there. Because of what happened to you, you may be too angry at your children or too sad to love. You may fear being intimate with your partner. You may be too afraid to challenge wrongdoers. You may easily fall into a rage or a depression.

You may have been too tempted to use drugs and alcohol to quiet your fears and soften your agony.

In Iconic therapy, you will be told that disclosure is the first step in the healing journey. It is a step that is required to help process and gain a deeper understanding of what happened. Generally, the disclosure will be an emotional experience and difficult to get through, especially when you are disclosing for the first time. If this is the case, do not be discouraged. You will be advised to pause and gather yourself, to breathe, and to push through, to say what should be said. If it is too hard, you will be told that your effort was a good one for the first time. You will be encouraged to try again in the next session. For those of you who struggle with verbalizing and are lost for words, you will be encouraged to bring your thoughts in writing and read them to your therapist. If you are in a group, maybe another member will help you prepare a written account of what happened. Then you will be encouraged to give it another try as a step in taking ownership of your history. Generally, a second effort at disclosing is not required, but occasionally it is. Sometimes, much later in the therapeutic process the client may say, "I want to do the disclosure again. I was too afraid to say it all the first time. Now I'm not so afraid. I want to work it all the way through."

Then the disclosure is heard again, with more detail. Sometimes, after a difficult disclosure, the disclosing person will be upset and feel unsettled for a day or two or even longer. This is part of the journey and the therapist must be willing to allow the suffering that is attached to the disclosure. It is a type of disintegration, where old structures in the personality are breaking up and being replaced. After suffering through the disclosure, you will find a sense of integrity, a coming together with your previously denied, minimized, and unexamined past. Eventually, this will lead to a physiological experience that is often expressed as "I feel lighter—not so heavy" or "it's brighter in here now."

Once you have shared your disclosure, the freedom train is moving, and you are on it! You are moving in the direction of personal freedom. Although the remaining exercises are difficult, the energy and commitment to do them is strengthened. Optimism, mixed with apprehension and excitement, will carry you forward to the next exercise.

For the Reader Contemplating Entering Iconic Therapy

I realize that it is frightening to even contemplate sharing your devastating experiences with anybody, but please remember that you cannot have a full life if you are denying or minimizing important aspects of your history. Do not allow yourself to accept counsel from the negative Icons within that tell you to keep the secrets of the past and encourage you to believe that your life has been destroyed or permanently diminished by those demeaning past events. Do not let your fears from the past subtract from or limit your ability to take on future challenges. You survived the abuses of the past. Congratulations! Now, do not let the aftermath of that horror—which often includes self-condemnation, secrecy, shame, and fear—limit your journey to the highest level of your functioning. If the thought of beginning makes you anxious or worried, then begin privately, by writing down in a journal your description of what occurred. Then, take the next step. Meet with a psychologist or counsellor and tell him or her that you have been reading this book, and you want to disclose some painful experiences from the past. (These strategies work in individual counselling as well.) The therapist will listen and support you, and you will be on the healing journey.

Once disclosure has been achieved, the next event in the journey of healing is to confront the Icon directly and expose the propaganda for what it is—lies.

CHAPTER 12
Step Two: Role Play

Mike, though many years have passed, I have never forgotten your name. I never forgot what you did to me, that night I was babysitting for you and your wife. Sally was her name. It was very late when the two of you came back from your outing. I remember the two of you were arguing. You were both drunk. I lay in the bed beside the crib that your son, Johnny, was sleeping in.

Do you remember that night, Mike? Because I do; I remember every detail: how the furniture sat, the colour of the carpet, the ceiling of white, the rain that hit the window, and the blackness of the night. Mike, I was 11 years old, and you took my innocence. You got in my bed, told me to be quiet or you'd hurt me—but you hurt me anyway. Your wife, passed out in the next room, your son asleep beside us, and you took my innocence. "Be quiet and tell no one, or I'll hurt you more," and I quietly whimpered. Then you heard a noise. You got up and went out of the bedroom. That night, Mike, after you left that room, I got up and crawled under the crib. I saw you come back. I hid there quietly. I was scared. You never did find me. I fell asleep under that crib. In the morning, I went back home.

Mike, I know you remember. I know what your wife thought because I would not babysit again for her. But you know what? If you are dead, then God has already dealt with you. If you are still alive, you live with this guilt. I just want you to know I never forgot. You terrorized, threatened, and raped me. I kept this a secret for a lot of years, but I have learned something. Mike, I no longer carry the darkness you instilled in me, because God has taught me how to forgive. So, just so you know, I have forgiven you. I pray that you can forgive yourself.

In Iconic therapy, the role play is a very difficult, probably the most difficult step in the healing journey. The woman who wrote the quote above and later spoke about her abusive experiences, still needed to complete the role play to find healing and release from her inner feelings of anger and injustice. The role play requires you to challenge and confront the abuse and disrespect that you have endured. These negative experiences often include parent abandonment, sexual or physical abuse, and a multitude of other forms of injustice. If the role play were to be weighed in terms of therapeutic progress, it would receive a weight of 50 percent. Another 25 percent of healing would be gained by the disclosure and 25 percent with the remaining exercises. For many, the role play is the most difficult exercise to complete. When you have completed it, you will experience a positive change in how you think about yourself and possibly a clearer understanding of those who have mistreated you.

As the victim of injustice, you often have little or no concept of how to address the deep concerns you carry within your personality: the haunting and hurtful memories that frequently invade your consciousness. Often, there is no safe opportunity for a confrontation/discussion with the person responsible for the injustice. As well, for many, the emotional release through disclosure (as discussed in the previous chapter) and the insight that followed was all that was expected or hoped for.

Going Beyond Disclosure to the Release of Emotions

The very thought of somehow going beyond the disclosure of past hurts and engaging in role play with a (symbolic) hurtful person from the past may seem too much for you. It may be just too difficult to imagine being asked to find the words to express and release feelings associated with the injustice that you have been trying to forget (deny) or diminish (minimize). In your guardedness, many of you will tell yourselves that the role-play exercise is excessive, possibly overwhelming, and unnecessary for you.

In spite of the promise of a good return for your effort at role-playing the confrontational scenario, you will find within yourself a natural, survival-oriented resistance to taking on this challenge. You will be bombarded within with many errors in thinking, which will advise against making this therapeutic effort. I encourage you to overcome those inner voices that discourage you from doing the role play—telling you that it is too late to change, that it is hopeless, that you are not good enough, and that it is not worth the anxiety you would have to endure. I will say this in response to your extreme reluctance: do not let your anxiety and fear direct your life in this instance.

If it is difficult to imagine doing the role play, it will obviously be difficult to do. Another way to think about it is to ask yourself, "Why is it so frightening?" It is because you have survived what occurred to you by putting yourself in flight mode, coping with the trauma by running from it, or minimizing it, or denying it. Please understand, I do not say this to belittle or demean your coping strategies. You reacted as you did because there were few options available for you. Remember, Iconic theory has its foundation set on survival energies. You reacted to the frightening events in an effort to survive, to maintain your life or, at a minimum, to maintain the integrity of your personality.

On the positive side, you did survive the abuse/trauma/injustice. What remains now is a somewhat dysfunctional personality clinging to deeply ingrained, flight-oriented, avoidant survival strategies that are no longer necessary. Because you are only reading this book and have made no commitments to do anything, please relax with the thought that the role play *might* be something that could assist you in your efforts to break free of whatever it is that is holding you back. You always have the option to conclude that this type of therapy is not for you. However, please know that I believe it will work for you if you commit yourself to just giving it a try. Even if you do not believe in the principles I base this exercise upon, if you try it anyway, it *will* work for you.

▶ Some comments for therapists

Role play is the primary therapeutic technique that separates Iconic therapy from most other forms of therapy. The principles used in the Iconic approach are unique, and thus the role play is structured in accordance with that uniqueness. As noted earlier, I have included special comments for therapists on how to direct and participate in the role play in Appendix 1.

▶ You may experience a strong resistance from within

As noted above, the power of the negative Icon within usually triggers a mindset that the role play, the confrontation with the Icon, will somehow lead to something you would rather not experience although it would occur in a safe and private setting with a trusted psychologist or counsellor. You may also think that you could do the exercise if you just willed yourself to accept the possibility that it could lead to something better. I encourage you to go with this second conclusion, to break from you old ways of thinking and reacting, to try something different.

To set aside these very practised strategies of keeping safe, of "not rocking the boat" is most likely very much out of character and upsetting for you. Please remember, you have been using survival strategies that support flight from the horror of what you have experienced, compliance with the destructiveness you have endured and reticence when you wanted to speak. These are now self-defeating strategies which limit your efforts to lead a full life and trigger you to re-experience feelings of anxiety, fear, shame, and sadness.

This is the key to understanding the dilemma of those who struggle with inner conflict from past horror or abuse. The Icon symbolizes the extremely upsetting event. Even though days, months, or years may have passed; even though you have matured, and you are no longer the younger person you were when you suffered through those terrible moments; even though the horrible memory of what occurred has lost some of its power or the key players have died or disappeared—you will still resist the symbolic confrontation, the role play. It is now time, after careful consideration, to change your approach.

You should also understand that the therapist is not going to play the part of the adversary exactly as it occurred for you. He or she will play this part in a manner that will allow it to be therapeutic. The role play scenario is designed to provide a platform for you to release all of the toxic emotions that remain for what occurred. When the therapist plays the part of the abuser/perpetrator as overwhelmed, confused, and apologetic, he is doing so to allow you to take a stronger stance than you have ever contemplated before. You may tell the therapist that he is not playing the part exactly as the perpetrator would, but he knows this. If he acted as the perpetrator, he most likely would be abusive and would try to crush you or shut you down. This could prevent you from finding your voice and would not be therapeutic. As well, please understand that if you refuse to engage totally in the role play because the therapist is not playing the part accurately, you may have an ulterior motive. By challenging the process of the role play, you may be surreptitiously avoiding the expression of your repressed emotions, as to find your voice within the role play may be frightening for you. Please do not get caught in the defensive excuse: "This exercise won't work because my abuser would never be like you." If you give yourself totally to its purpose - to release your true voice and express deeply felt but long-suppressed emotions - the role-play exercise will be very healing for you.

That Memory Has the Power to Limit You

For those of you who struggle with these negative Icons (and that is most of us), you are still visited by the fleeting perception that the event itself and the horrible outcome that followed have all the power and you have none. During moments of stress, you still believe the Iconic echo, that voice within that visits you often at a deeper level to remind you, "You are not deserving of any other outcome. It really was your fault. The die is cast. Your life will never be the same. You are doomed to unhappiness."

You still believe the lies and distortions you tell yourself every day as a means of coping: "It's not that bad. I'm over it. My addiction to alcohol/drugs/sex/food is not about that. My lingering depression, my temper tantrums and my inability to love have nothing to do with it."

It is easy to understand then, why you may feel tempted to resist taking part in the role play. Logic, gentle coaxing, and the examples of others who have previously completed the role play are the tools that will be used to encourage you to overcome those inner voices of resistance, resignation, and self-defeat. With gentleness and respect, you will be encouraged to understand that this is the way out of that inner conflict.

Here are comments from a client written when preparing for the role play exercise:

> *David: Hi, do you remember me? It's ... You stole my innocence and then laughed at me. Is this ringing any bells for you? It has been 13 years now—a long time. How do you sleep at night? Well, for 13 years, I have been hurt, lost, embarrassed, and felt like a whore, all on account of your sick, selfish, inhumane actions. How can you look at yourself in the mirror daily knowing you stole a little girl's innocence? Stole something from her that was so precious and irreplaceable? For 13 years, I have felt like a whore and bottled up those sick memories, but it's time I told you how I felt. I think you are a waste of skin. I wish nothing more than for you to feel what I have all these years, but that would make me fall to your level. I am not going to waste another ounce of sorrow on you, because you are dead to me. One day, you'll have to face what you did in front of God, and that is satisfaction for me. You are nothing and always will be nothing! That is all I have to say to you.*

The next example was written after the role play (by another client):

> *The impact of the role play gave me empowerment. It gave me the opportunity to say what I wanted—to tell him, "I told on you, and they believed me. Now someone knows!" But I was also able to tell him, "I forgive you," so I no longer would ever feel the burden he laid on me as a little girl again. It was after this stage I started to really gain some insight into my issues and behaviors, the causes and effects.*

Many of you who are reading this will feel uneasy and mildly anxious. You know that you are carrying an unresolved problem from the past and that an Icon lives within you. You are not alone. The truth is, it happens to all of us. After reading the comments above, you may feel that you would avoid that role play. Please remember that the message to avoid the role play is coming from the propaganda in your mind that limits you and distorts your thinking. I am only suggesting an exercise that will release you from the hold of that propaganda. The exercise will not kill you; it will strengthen you. It will free you.

I encourage you to take on the challenge. Lift your eyes from this book and imagine the role play that you should do. Imagine speaking to that person who hurt you; imagine saying those things that should be said to the person who sexually, physically, emotionally, verbally assaulted you or abandoned you or died before they should have. I know you feel anxiety rising within, even when you contemplate such a thing. That is the anxiety that is triggered in your life when you face potential abusers, unfairness, and/or the loss of loved ones. That is the anxiety that keeps you from the full life and the full commitment to be the passionate person you aspire to become. That is the anxiety that will leave you once you have completed this program.

It is time to take the next step. Arrange to meet with a psychologist or counsellor, tell him or her that you are ready to take on the role play, and ask for help with this exercise. There is a good chance that you will find a clarity you have never known.

Most victims of trauma or profound loss have never confronted their issues in role play. In certain situations, such as sexual abuse, if the thought of confronting the perpetrator has been entertained, it often includes an extreme fantasy to kill the perpetrator or beat him badly. Many in the Iconic therapy program had extreme anger that was very close to the surface. They were often legitimately afraid of their anger. The anger for their abusers was so intense that it had already manifested in destructive conflict with others.

Some of the participants were in jail for aggravated assault; some had stabbed their adversaries. They were often realistically afraid of their anger and feared that it would be released aggressively and inappropriately in the role play. I have heard the following on more than one occasion: "If I were to do the role play, I would lose control and hurt you or beat you. You don't want to see me when I'm that angry."

In Iconic therapy, the relationship you have with the Icon in your mind is exposed, and you are encouraged to find the words you would like to say about how much or in what ways you were hurt by an experience from the past. When first contemplating such an endeavor, you may have very little understanding regarding the nature of your anger and the sadness that is also present. You may struggle greatly to express it in words. It may be that the trauma was so damaging or frightening at the time of its occurrence that there was never a thought nor a mental rehearsal of what could be said. Quite possibly you may have never considered how to formulate your feelings in words. If the horrible event occurred at a very young age, the memory and its attached emotion are often stored in a preverbal format and have not been translated to language. Whatever the explanation, the solution begins by retrieving the memory, expressing it verbally, and then restructuring that same memory by adding the confrontation in present-day language. Finally, when the role play is completed, the memory is re-filed, in a new form, with a different ending—the confrontation. Even though symbolic, the role play requires the actualization of valid (long-suppressed) emotions. This actualizing experience will place a different emotional dynamic on the memory trace and will alter your understanding and memory of the traumatic event.

If, like many clients, you are totally at a loss as to what should be said in the role-playing exercise, you will be encouraged to delay the role play and prepare before the next meeting by thinking about and then, if you believe it would be helpful, writing about what should be said from your perspective. Often the victims of horrible events are very proficient at writing, but when it comes to speaking the painful feelings in the role play, they are overwhelmed. Translating from one modality, writing, to another, speaking, is an important and essential step.

In an effort to help you find the words that you long to release, the truth about the pain you experienced, your therapist might discuss with you, especially if you are struggling, what could be said during the role play. The therapist might say:

> "Would this be true for you? 'It really hurt me—what you did. You had no right to do that. Why would you do that?'"

Or, if you are suffering with the suicide of a loved one, the therapist might say,

> "Would this be true for you? 'It has been so difficult for me to live in a world when you are not here. It is not right and—I am angry at you. How could you do that and leave me with all that pain?'"

These statements, planted like seeds, may trigger deeply rooted concerns that you want addressed. For many, the primary concern is the need for an explanation. You might want to ask, "Why did you do that?" You may also find that you have strong feelings of anger and disgust: "I hated what you did." Further, you may realize an inner sense of betrayal. "How could you do that to me? I trusted you and loved you."

The source of each person's deep pain is unique, but the release of that pain tends to follow common themes:

- a longing to understand the motivation underlying the horrible event ("Why did you do it?");
- a need to express the pain it caused ("It hurt me, and it still hurts");

- a longing to release the anger you still hold ("I'm angry at you");
- a need to share your conclusion that you believe you were betrayed ("You were not supposed to do that"); and, finally,
- a need to express your inner sense of condemnation for their action ("I will never forgive you").

When these themes are addressed and the words that capture the essence of your inner feelings are finally stated to the (symbolic) perpetrator you will experience a sense of release and an alignment with your true self. You will no longer feel divided about what happened to you; no longer in a conflict about your role in the abuse scenario. You will finally accept that not only were you taken advantage of but also that you have finally addressed the injustice. Finally you will be at home and comfortable with your true self. You will begin to experience a feeling of integration, a coming together within yourself.

Observing Others

It will be extremely helpful for you to observe someone else completing the role-play exercise. For many of you, even the thought of confronting the difficult situation is shocking, almost unconscionable. You may even be very uncomfortable when you observe others doing what you believe you could never do. It will be a struggle to even consider doing such a thing. The observer who has not completed the role play will often cry when another tries theirs. Afterwards, the novice observer is often amazed, confused, and frightened by what has been seen and heard. That is why, if you have read this far, I know that you are now coming to the inner belief that it is something that you could do—and you are right. It is not that dangerous and you can do it if you choose.

Crying Is Okay

Sometimes people cry during the role play. In most cases, however, the words come more easily than you would expect. Generally, it has been my practice to allow candidates to struggle with what they want to say and if tears flow that is part of it. I tend to not give answers or to disallow feelings of any nature. As well, it is important to understand that each client's pain is unique. For example, one client's main theme may center on the motivation factor ("Why would you do such a thing?"), while another may focus on betrayal ("A father should never do that").

A Letter Might Help

Sometimes clients will write letters (that will not be sent) in an effort to prepare for the role play as a letter can serve as a catalyst for the confrontation that will follow. This is a letter to an abusive father, written in preparation for role play:

> *Dear Dad[9],*
>
> *Hey, how are you, Dad? There is a purpose as to why I'm writing this letter, not just a friendly hello—that too, though. Dad, I have been doing quite a bit of work on myself over the past year or so ... When in recovery, you are encouraged to dig deep within ... Dad, a major issue from my past is when I was sexually abused by you. Just now, at age 24, I am ready, as well as willing, to deal with the emotional scarring and the effects it has had on my entire life. It has affected me in more ways than one.*

---

[9] Each letter is very personal and all of the details and questions asked in this letter may not be necessary in your letter and should not be considered essential.

There are a few questions I want to ask you, to get them off my chest! Dad, please listen to them, and when you are honestly able to answer, I'd very much appreciate an answer.

Dad, how old was I when you began to abuse me? Do you remember what happened the first time? Dad, why did you want to touch me and play with my privates? Were you attracted to me? When did you realize you were sexually attracted to your daughter? Was it when you first began the sexual abuse? Or did you want to do it before, but never did? How did you get the courage to first touch me? Dad, were you sexually abused? If so, who sexually abused you? Did you feel guilty at all by sexually abusing me? Or was it all fine and dandy to you? Dad, do you remember how long the abuse continued? Do you remember that last time? What happened to make you stop? Dad, did you do it to anyone else? Or was it just me? Dad, what do you think when you see me now? What thoughts cross your mind? Do you remember and envision the abuse when you see me? Do you ever think about it? Is there anything you would like to say to me?

Dad, if there is anything you want to talk to me about, please do. I am working on this for my sake. It totally helps to deal with such deep feelings that for so long have been buried deeper and deeper. Almost to a point of forgetting, but really not quite; it's always been there. This sexual abuse from you, Dad, was a traumatic experience in my life that happened over and over. My inner child was scarred for life and is afraid, terrified, and very traumatized. Through all the sexual abuse, it may have not seemed like a big deal to you, but to me it was. Dad, you stole my innocence. I felt dirty, used, abused, and guilty. I felt weird, different, and very confused. I felt strange and yet loved in a sense. I was getting attention, but not in a healthy way a child should. Dad, did you know the sexual abuse you put me through is still with me now at age 24 and will continue to be until I choose to break free and let go? I can do that, I'm learning how to, and it feels great. Dad, this is not my guilt to carry; never was I in the wrong—never! It was your fault, Dad; your selfishness has torn a part from me that just now I am beginning to heal from. Dad, I was scared and in fear of Mom knowing and how much it would hurt her. I never wanted to hurt my Mommy; she would cry, and then so would I, because I loved my Mom. I was scared for Sally, too, but kept silent. I never wanted to tear our family apart. I always wanted a close and loving family; I felt that we had that despite this dark secret. Dad, I was not trying to protect you by not telling. I was trying to protect Mom and Sally and me. Dad, when our family sat down this summer and the sexual abuse was confronted, how did you feel? Threatened, scared, or worried? Dad, why did you deny it and say nothing happened and made me look like a liar? Honestly, Dad. Because, then there you were, all of a sudden admitting it to Mom and Sally and me too. Dad, I do forgive you. I just needed some closure with you by answering these questions on paper or in person. We are both adults, and this has a great deal to do with my recovery and my past life.

Please respect my recovery and respond honestly. Dad, do you love me? Do you think that you have a problem? Are you willing to seek counselling and get help for yourself? I am having a baby, Dad, and you will be a grandpa—but how can I trust you with my child or even being around my child? If you are willing to seek help and answer my questions, it would go a long way in building trust.

Thanks, Dad. I love you.

Writing a letter can serve as an excellent step to prepare for the role play. However, I believe the letter alone is often not enough. It will help but for complete healing, the words, thoughts, and feelings in the letter should be expressed within the role play. In that modality, the integration of thoughts and feelings occurs. If one only writes the letter, the solution tends to be in the head and not in the heart—and it is in the heart where the pain and suffering reside.

Should You Confront the Actual Perpetrator?

Another point that I often explain to the client doing the role play involves the nature of their present relationship with the perpetrator. Let us say, for this example, that the stepfather is the abusive person. The client may say, "I don't want to confront him—he is a very dangerous person. He might kill me." The therapist would then reply in this way:

> This exercise is about your personal development. It is not about him and the way he is. We don't know what he would do. It is not our advice to necessarily confront this person in real life. You do not confront someone if they are carrying a machine gun. You do not confront when your life is at risk. In this room, you are safe. This symbolic confrontation is part of your healing journey, to finally prepare you to stand up to fear, to stand up to abusive people you will meet in the future, to allow your fear and anger a voice to

address the abuses of your past. Once you complete the role play, you will begin to see yourself as a person who will not tolerate abuse. You will give off the aura of a strong and confident person with well-defined boundaries. You will no longer present, or think of yourself as vulnerable, as a victim. That is the purpose of the exercise.

Here is another example of written material. This woman was preparing for the role play with an uncle who had sexually abused her. She later spoke the words in her role play.

John,

All I want to know is why. Why did you do those things to me when Mom was at bingo? John, why did you send the other kids out to play, and I was not allowed? I had to stay in then, and then you would tell me to have a bath. I didn't want to, but you told me to. That was when you would hurt me. You always told me not to tell or you would send me away, and I would never see my mommy again. I hated you for that, John! Why would you buy me stuff and give me money? Did you do it so I wouldn't tell—you know I didn't like that stuff. I used to wash myself and scrub till I would bleed because you would make me feel so dirty. You made me hate myself, John. Even when I did tell Mom, you would still touch me—why, John? Why did you do that to me? I was just a child, and you took my childhood away from me, and I hate you for that. You kept hurting me till I was 12 years old. Why? Why did you do that to me? Please tell me why you took my life away.

Even though these thoughts and feelings were well written in the letter, it is important to understand that each step in the therapeutic process matters. To write these sentiments is a good beginning, and to read them out loud to the therapist is a good second stage of expression—but the ultimate resolving and releasing effort is that of offering these same thoughts and feelings within the back-and-forth exchange of the role play. When these same thoughts and feelings are expressed within the dynamic of the role play, a much more powerful release of the repressed, toxic emotions occurs, along with a greater sense of resolution and completeness.

In role plays that involve sexual and physical abuse, clients come to understand the selfish motives of the abuser and to see the abuser as filled with personal problems. He is now seen as selfish. He took what he wanted for selfish reasons. His actions were not motivated by the victim of his actions but rather by his own needs. It was not about you. If you are the victim of abuse, you will gain a better perspective on issues of responsibility and come to understand at a deeper level that you were not responsible for the assault, whether it was sexual, physical, or verbal. As a consequence, you as the victim will begin to acquire a clearer understanding that what occurred was not your fault, and you will finally realize and more importantly accept that it was not your actions that led to the terrible events that you experienced.

Here is another letter of a terribly traumatic event that had to be dealt with in role play for a resolution to be found. When this woman was eight years old, she witnessed her mother kill her father. With the successful completion of this very difficult role play in a riveting group therapy session, she was able to finally release her deep sense of anger. What follows is what she wrote after the difficult role play and Cloak of Shame exercise.

> *Hello, my name is ... I am a mother of four baby girls ...*
> *I want to say thank you to all you wonderful women who*
> *were and are still in the Courage of Women program, who*

let me cry and gave me a tissue. It really helped ... I was so focused on the wonderful feeling [after the role play] when I left that room, the joy and the happiness. Anyways, I have been in this program for two years and working on these issues that are no longer mine. I want to say that I was only eight or nine when my mother killed my dad in front of me, and my brother and I watched him suffer. It was the most horrible feeling ever. All he [the father] said was "run" and that he loved me, and at that time, I was afraid and angry towards my mom. I thought only to keep my brother safe and threw him out the window. We ran, like he said to do. But for so long [20 years], I held on to the anger and hate. I sometimes got her [the mother, after she was released from jail] drunk so I could confront her. But we all ended up too drunk, so it was not the time ...

It helped me a lot [the role play], even to a point where the last day I came to Courage of Women and cried so much I was shaking, I called my mom and guess what? She booked a visit and came here and told me she was sorry face to face and told me how much she loves me. I was so upset, but it was awesome later, because it surely was this program, that helped me, and now I'm going home soon. I feel very glad I left my sadness on the Cloak of Shame ... I'm not afraid to cry. Its okay to let these feelings go, 'cause I should know, growing up in anxiety attacks and anger. Anyways, thanks to all you wonderful people. I will not ever forget and will always remember.

This was one of the most powerful role plays I had ever witnessed. As I observed it, I knew, and all present in the group knew, that this lady was finally saying what had to be said for her to find and release her true self. The successful resolution of this extremely abusive experience supports the basic principle of Iconic therapy, namely that these traumatic experiences are often best dealt with in a therapeutic setting with a role play that will allow the client to release the repressed feelings. As noted in her story, she tried and failed in real life with her mother to say what should be said. In their drunkenness, the words and the feelings that would release the pain and sorrow within could not be found. She had carried anger and rage from the age of eight, and these feelings would be triggered, especially by women with whom she was in conflict. (She had numerous convictions for assault.) But the release of her anger and violence towards others would only give her temporary relief, while adding a layer of guilt. Using the Iconic approach, the true release of the repressed emotions was finally achieved. This can happen for all of us. Our inner Icons may not be as overwhelming as hers, but they are still there. They still restrict us. We can take them on in the role play, as this very courageous lady did.

Role Play to Cope with Your Loss of a Loved One

I also completed a role play with this same lady to assist her with the loss of her murdered father. This same approach can be used in similar circumstances in individual counselling.

A young man who had lost two important people in his life to suicide was referred to me. He wrote about the impact of these very unfortunate events.

> In the past couple of years my life took a turn around and my world as I knew it was flipped upside down. ... I had just turned 21 years old ... and my long-time friend since elementary school made a decision that not only affected me and his family but many of our friends. I stumbled across a scene that I still try to wipe from my memory. My best friend decided to take his life that day with one shot

> *from his hand gun. After ... I didn't speak much about it.*
> *I began to shut down my emotions. By the next summer ...*
> *my father who was my next best friend attempted suicide.*
> *He was unsuccessful but within the next month he was*
> *finally successful. I not only began blaming myself for*
> *everything but began to shut my emotions and any feelings*
> *of realness completely off. ... I began to speak with a*
> *psychologist.*

In five sessions we completed the disclosures and the two role plays, one with his best friend the other with his father. These were his written comments afterwards.

> *I felt like a glass doll that had been smashed. We were*
> *able to carefully glue the pieces back together. Slowly the*
> *cracks are healing. With every session [which included the*
> *role plays] my positive emotions were turned back on. I*
> *began to feel much more alive and began to find love in*
> *my heart to share with my family. As we spoke it was as*
> *though every word and sentence was a weight lifted out*
> *of this backpack of weight that began to build since it all*
> *happened. Before I knew it the only weight left was the*
> *weight of rebuilding my life and the many years I look*
> *forward to as a young adult at the age of 23.*

The role plays that were required to generate this type of profound change served as the catalyst to a deeper level of insight and acceptance. Once the role plays were completed participants found that they were not so easily triggered to mentally return to the memories of death and loss that had continually haunted them. Finally their inner sense of rage, frustration, anger and sadness had been released. The exercises and conversations that followed and their written commentary brought them much closer to a final sense of resolution and letting go.

For those of you who have experienced the tragic loss of a loved one, I realize that reading these passages will be difficult. I encourage you to face the horrible tragedy you have endured and recover from it. There are others in your life that need your love, support, and affection. There is a time for grieving and then a time to set that aside. The loss of a cherished and precious loved one to sudden death is a terrible thing. But your life is precious too, and you need to turn from the past to continue your journey. To the clients struggling with tragedies of this nature, with the deepest of respect, I say this:

> Please do not let the murder or suicide of your loved one destroy your soul as well. Do not get lost in thinking that you are the only one. Many have suffered these tragedies, especially during wartime. Do not succumb to the error in thinking that says, "My life has been ruined by the death of my loved one. Somehow it was my fault. I cannot release myself from the sadness of it all." Do not give up your essence. Trust me. You can overcome these horrible events.

In my experiences in the prison system, I worked with many who had lost loved ones to suicide and murder. I was honored to remind them of the truth:

> You know that your lost loved one would want you to carry on with even greater commitment to life than before, to live for them as well as for you.

Successfully completing the role play will allow you to gain insight into the nature of your suffering and release you from it. It will also allow you to understand the suffering and sorrow of others.

If you were the indirect victim of violence, who lost a loved one to murder or suicide or to an accident, then the role play with that person or persons who ended the life of your loved one will help you express and release your anger for the deep sense of injustice you hold within. It will help you connect with and let go of the sadness for your loss. Further, when you speak (in a second role play) directly to the lost loved one, you will finally have found a place where you can express the deep love you still feel for that treasured person you hold in your heart. Finally, you will be willing to allow the shame to lift, the shame from believing that somehow the loss was your fault, when it never was.

Once you have completed the role play (or role plays), you will be ready to move forward to the next level, a much easier exercise and almost joyful experience—the Cloak of Shame.

CHAPTER 13
Step Three: Releasing the Shame That Covers You

When you have successfully completed the difficult disclosure and role-play exercises you will then slowly begin to understand that you are a person of worth and dignity. These exercises will have diminished your Iconic echo ("You're not good enough") and your Iconic reaction ("I'll never have the life I want; I won't even try"). These same exercises, once completed, will begin breaking the hold of many errors in thinking ("I'm not good enough - I deserved it all"). However, the feelings of shame attached to the original trauma have an enduring negativity that often remains. Even though you now realize that you do not deserve the shame, you will often still carry it. This lingering shame feeds and encourages depression and discouragement when you are involved in the challenges of everyday life. The primary feeling deep down ("I feel ashamed. I feel unworthy") needs to be eradicated. You have been carrying this shame for an extended period, possibly for years. Apart from the trauma, the shame itself needs a special and direct attack to break its stranglehold.

The Cloak of Shame Exercise

Most victims of trauma carry shame. Traditional "talk therapies" will be helpful in addressing the trauma at a cognitive (in the head) level, but the shame may continue at the core of the psyche (in the heart). After the difficult role-play experience, you will be asked whether you would like to take part in the Cloak of Shame exercise. Most find this task rather easy, as it is an exercise that requires very little speaking on your part. It is mostly a feeling exercise. You will be asked to stand in the middle of the group or, in individual therapy, in front of your therapist. A black cloak with a large hood will be carefully placed over your shoulders. You will be asked permission to have the hood fall over your face, so that you are entirely cloaked in symbolic shame. (Some individuals, who have been traumatized when asleep and in the dark, do not want their faces covered. This is allowed. This is an indication that one aspect of their abusive past remains unresolved and should be dealt with on a latter occasion.) Once you are cloaked, the therapist will then place his hands on your shoulders, applying some pressure, to symbolize the weight of the shame. You will then be asked if you have been carrying shame related to the unfairness you have endured. Something like the following will be heard:

Therapist:	Laura, have you been carrying the shame of being sexually abused by your uncle when you were five years old?
Or:	John, have you been carrying shame for the suicide death of your wife?
Or:	Jim, have you been carrying shame for the loss of your comrade in the Afghanistan conflict?
Or:	James, have you been carrying shame for failing to meet the expectations of an overly demanding father?
Laura:	Yes.
Therapist:	Do you deserve to be carrying shame for being a part of what happened, when you were five years old?
Laura:	No. I don't deserve to carry this shame. I want to get rid of it.

Therapist: Do you realize that shame is not yours—that shame belongs to your uncle?

Laura: Yes, it's his shame.

Then the therapist says to the entire group:

Therapist: Does Laura deserve to carry shame for being abused, starting at the age of five? She was only five years old. She was innocent. She kept quiet to protect her family. Should she continue to carry this shame?

Group: No. You don't deserve to carry it. It's his shame. Take off the cloak of shame. Stomp on it.

Therapist: Cast off the cloak of shame and feel the freedom of a life without shame. Stomp on that cloak.

You will then remove the cloak of shame, kick at it, and jump on it! Sometimes others will spontaneously jump on it. There is usually an element of joy in the moment. Then you will be congratulated, and the exercise will end with the therapist's comments:

'Laura, that cloak of shame that you didn't deserve to carry has been cast off. You should have never been abused and you no longer need to carry shame for being part of what happened. How do you feel?' Often the response is: 'I feel lighter' and the therapist will reply – 'The weight of that shame is no longer on your shoulders. You never deserved it, and now it's finally gone.'

Here are comments from women in the Courage of Women program who completed the Cloak of Shame exercise.

When I did the Cloak of Shame, I was surprised how well it worked. It's dark in there. You listen to Dr. Pugh's voice talk about the guilt and shame. You feel it just as much as you feel his hands on your shoulders. When that cloak comes off, I felt new, somehow.

Guilt and shame have been such a big part of my life. It feels amazing when they lift. I know I have a long way to go before I truly feel no guilt or shame over this, but a big weight has been lifted.

I was able to let go of all the shame, guilt, pain, and any other feelings that had burdened me for so many years— the Cloak of Shame—I cast off—stomped and kicked. I will never allow myself to feel inadequate or let that "yucky" feeling bother me anymore. I was done.

It's not that everything is all hunky-dory because I shed a cloak. It just made me know I was healing. I have a new strength and a new hope. I am not sure what I'll find next on my journey. I feel I will concentrate to gain more strength as I try to encourage those who come after me to travel the journey to heal, letting them know that there is hope and that courage can be gained with each step they take.

The Chant

Sometimes a chant is used to set up and introduce the Cloak of Shame exercise. The chant repeats a theme that runs counter to the error in thinking that many victims of trauma carry, namely, "I feel ashamed for having been part of what happened." The chant can also move even the quietest member of the group to begin to verbalize what they suspect is the truth, a truth that they could never have said out loud before. The chant I have been using is primarily for those seen in a group program who have been sexually, physically, and verbally abused.

Leader:	We are now going to do the "chant." That will set us up for the Cloak of Shame exercise that we have planned. I am going to say statements that are true, and I want you to say them right after me.
Leader:	If you believe the shame of the abuse belongs to the abuser, say, "The shame is theirs."
Group:	The shame is theirs.
Leader:	Can you say, "The shame is not mine"?
Group:	The shame is not mine.
Leader:	Now, stand up (pause) and say it with conviction!
Group:	The shame is not mine!
Leader:	Now, can each of you say it like this—using your own name: "I'm Kathy, and the shame is not mine," followed by a group chorus: "She's Kathy, and the shame is not hers." Let's start with Kathy. Kathy say, "I'm Kathy, and the shame is not mine."
Kathy:	I'm Kathy, and the shame is not mine.
Group:	She's Kathy, and the shame is not hers.
Leader:	[to the next in the group] And now Lea.
Lea:	I'm Lea, and the shame is not mine.
Group:	She's Lea, and that shame is not hers.
	And so on ...

The chant is a very easy exercise that all can take part in without commitment to do more. However, I have seen participants cry during this exercise, somehow relieved to speak the truth out loud—that they do not deserve to carry shame for what was forced upon them.

This exercise will allow you to hear the supportive chorus of the group reminding you that you do not deserve to carry shame anymore. (I do not use the chant during individual counselling as it needs the group and the chorus.)

Once the Cloak of Shame and the Chant have been completed, you will be ready to move forward to the next level, that of being an advocate for victims who have suffered similar types of injustice.

CHAPTER 14
Steps Four and Five: Advocating

Step 4: Advocacy in the Program

Once you have completed at least the disclosure and the role-play portion of the program, you are encouraged (or you will volunteer) to serve as a spokesperson for the program. In this capacity, you will welcome a new person to the program, introduce yourself and the therapists, and relate the structure and expectations within the program (i.e., confidentiality, respect, honesty). As an advocate, you will be encouraged to use your own participation in the program as an example of how to proceed, taking ownership of your own abuse, but this time for a different reason. You will use the acknowledgement of your difficult experiences from the past ("I was sexually abused by my stepfather, and this program has helped me") in a manner that will be helpful to others. Then you will explain the exercises that are part of the process. Usually the remarks will be along this line:

> Welcome to the group. I'm Angela, and I have been coming to this group for three weeks. It is a group about courage. I was sexually abused by my uncle and my brother from age five to twelve. I never talked about it before I came here. You start with the disclosure; that is, you tell about whatever happened to you. Then, you do role play with the abuser, telling the person

who hurt you (played by Dr. Pugh) what you really think about what he did. Then, there is the Cloak of Shame, where you wear your shame and then remove it. It is really a neat experience. Then, there are other exercises. I haven't done them all yet. There is being an advocate, that's what I'm doing now—introducing you and advocating for the program. Then there is the Speech to the Community, where you talk to a group in the community about what happened to you, in a way trying to heal the community. After that is the Breaking Free exercise. You will hear more about that later.

Please remember, you don't have to do anything when you are here. It is all voluntary. It can be pretty scary when you start. I know; I was afraid, but it has been great for me. I love this program.

Oh yes, one final thing. We have three rules: First, respect—please respect the other group members. When they are talking or doing an exercise, don't interrupt them or speak over them. Second, honesty— we try to be honest. If something is too hard, you can say, "I don't want to talk about that," or "I'm not ready to deal with that," or "I'm not ready yet." You are never forced here to do anything. Third, confidentiality for the group members—you are not allowed to go back to the unit and talk about anything another person said. What is said here is private, and we expect you to respect that privacy. For the group leaders, the rules are different for them. If they think you might harm yourself or others, then they have to take action to protect anyone in danger. If you mention in your story that a child in the community might be in danger, they will want to take action to protect that child.

The advocacy exercise serves several purposes. First it allows the newcomer to feel welcomed by someone who is just like them. As well, once you have progressed to the advocacy level, it allows you to speak and to experience a new sense of self; you express yourself as a person who is healing from the abuse, a person who can take ownership of the past without being overwhelmed with shame. It also allows you to take on the role of nurturer and to use your abuse experience in a positive way. When you can advocate for what you know in your heart is right, you are taking steps in the direction of personal growth, even when this is not your primary purpose.

Group members are also encouraged to advocate for the program and its principles in their everyday life. In the jail setting, they are encouraged to tell others about the program and invite them to attend. At this stage, instead of being ashamed of their abuse, they are proud of their accomplishments to date and use their experience in a positive way to educate others.

True recovery from trauma is indicated when you speak out against what occurred to you in a public way, in an effort to heal others and to bring knowledge and healing to the community. This simple credo holds for individual counselling as well, although it is more difficult to implement. The individual client is encouraged, when there is an opportunity, to speak about the abusive experience they endured to a person they trust who might be helped by hearing about that experience and, as well, how to deal with it.

This effort to help others will allow you, the victim, to consolidate your progress and to take on a new role: understanding and assisting others who suffer from similar concerns. Being an advocate leads naturally to the next exercise, the Speech to the Community.

Step 5: Speech to the Community

This exercise involves taking part in a role play in which you are asked to imagine yourself addressing a group in the community.

When you read this, you may think, "I hate making speeches" or "I'm too nervous to do such a thing." However, you will be surprised with how easily you will be able to complete this exercise. The five earlier exercises (i.e., Disclosure, Role Play, Cloak of Shame, Chant, and Advocate) are so difficult and so empowering that once they are completed, you will discover that your voice has been freed and you are able to speak with a sincerity and honesty that you have never known. Ideally, in this exercise you will explain to a group in the community (symbolized by the other group members) that you endured a very negative experience. You will speak about the impact that experience has had upon you and how you now realize that it is important that certain initiatives be taken to protect others in the community from similar experiences. The primary objective of the speech is an effort to heal the community, to address concerns beyond your personal needs, and to attend to the needs of the community, with a focus on prevention. Some role play a speech to a class of elementary school children; others symbolically address the town council in their community.

Generally, when you do this exercise, you will write your speech and read it to the group. The speech is usually very brief, but occasionally more prolific writers will complete a longer speech. All speeches are received with a round of applause.

The exercise allows you to imagine, as part of your newly developing self, speaking out to defend those who have been hurt in a manner similar to the way you were hurt. As in the advocacy exercise described earlier in this chapter, you are encouraged to use the example of the injustices you experienced in a positive way to help the community. You will take your devastating experience and use it to inform and enlighten those in the community. This will help them learn of the horrors you endured so that they will be inspired to join with you in trying to prevent such tragedy happening again—to them or members of their families. The exercise allows you to think of yourself as a protector of others. You will begin to think, for example, about how parents should advise their children regarding situations where children might be at risk.

Here is an example of a Speech to the Community where women in general are addressed:

I am Joan … and here's my speech to the community.

This program of Courage of Women is to bring back the courage to abused women who have had emotion, trust, dignity, whatever it may be, stolen from them. It's different for each and every woman.

The counselling of Courage of Women helps restore all that women like us have been robbed of. It's up to you to have to want the healing exercises that are provided and use them to open up to yourself, so that we can help other women like us heal and live life in comfort and trust. So, we can be the role models as heroes to our children and generations to come; to let our perpetrators know that we are not defeated, that we still have our strength to walk in pride with our heads high, without shame. So we can be advocates to others, men or women, to let them know that there is help out there. There are people who care about what happened, who would like to point us in the right direction to healing, because they want us to be strong and not to continue to abuse our bodies with drugs and alcohol. We tend not to think about the emotional and mental abuse we are doing to our child or children by not being there.

So I would encourage women, and the women here today, to take the tools that we are offered. So we can break free of the shame that we all carry. So in the future, we can reflect on this moment with pride and strength, that we've been through a dark journey that needed light, and it was the strength that we have in our hearts that brought the light. Sunshine needs light, and smiles come from sunshine, and our children need our smiles to know that they are safe and can be happy, without living in fear the way we did.

What follows is a second example of a Speech to the Community, which was given a title:

When Trust Is Lost

There is healing for victims of sexual abuse, and there is still hope for you and me. I struggled with the damage of sexual abuse. You might wonder at this point if there really is hope for you. You might wonder if you could ever go through the process of facing the truth and embracing sorrow, choosing serenity, and pursuing love to the point of even forgiving the abuser.

Along with many others, you might ask why I should go through all that pain when I am happy today. I never found closure about my abuse and needed to work on it, so that is why I am here today. I am trying to get help on how to work on my abuse, so that I can go on with my everyday life, so that I can have a loving relationship with my husband, and so that we can have a healthy, happy sex life. I no longer want to be thinking about any of this when we are being intimate together. I am here today because I am working on myself and giving a voice to my inner child.

I have a lot of hope for myself and you can too!

Theoretically, as part of the journey of healing, those who complete all of the exercises will find their voices. This is one of the fundamental signs of personal growth—the belief that not only do you have a voice, but also that you should use that voice in speaking about your concerns. Here is an example of that sentiment:

> *I would love for women to have the courage to speak out, to have the voice that they have lost. I would love to be the teacher of what I've learned, and that is to forgive myself for thinking that it was me to blame. I want the women to know that we have courage to let it be heard—we are not to blame, and we carry no shame in the life we've lived and that we can forgive the people that made us feel that way.*
>
> *I want the women to hear that my voice has courage to teach and the courage to forgive, for I am a woman with courage, once again.*

I have added these two additional Speeches to the Community as examples, to honor these woman who have worked so hard:

> *Hello. My name is ... and I am no longer a victim without a voice. Today, I would like to address all the strong, proud, courageous, beautiful women out there, with the voice inside themselves, to speak out against the abuse that they have endured; in other words—all of you ... One of my most valuable things I've learned in life is this ... and I'm proud to be the one to share it with you—a fact that has changed my life forever—the shame is not mine! And it's not yours, either. I have found the courage inside myself to break through the anger, pain, and hurt buried within me, and you can too. Let the strong, positive, real you shine through. I have found my voice and will speak*

out loud and clear. No woman should ever live in fear. Embrace your voice, and tell your story. Each of us was made for glory.

I encourage all of you who have suffered injustice that continues to haunt you to begin the preparation in your mind, to form the words and sentences that will take your pain and transform it into a healing energy.

CHAPTER 15
Step Six: Breaking Free

The next to-last exercise In the program is Breaking Free. The purpose of this exercise is to consolidate gains and clarify your purpose and direction regarding the journey forward. It is an elaborate psychodrama that takes more quick thinking on the part of the therapist than any of the previous exercises. The focus of this exercise is to have you physically and symbolically face each of the barriers that have held you back from being the person you would like to be. (It was developed in the group therapy format but I have used it during individual counselling as well.)

The exercise begins by having you step forward to stand before the therapist. Then, for the group therapy approach, the other group members are called to stand behind you and show their support by placing their hands on your back. Next, the other group members are asked to voice their comments of support. You are then asked to turn and face the barriers that have held you back. The primary barriers are the ones you have already faced in the earlier exercises, with the main Iconic figures taken from the role plays that you have already completed (e.g., the abuser, the non-supporting parent, the abusive husband). One additional barrier is added that you have not dealt with previously in this program, that being the addictions barrier.

The barriers are represented by the pairing of group members, each pair holding hands to form a barrier. The therapist speaks for each barrier and asks the participant to respond before breaking through. This exercise is similar to the Cloak of Shame in that it is highly symbolic. It is like the "changing of the guard;" you replace the Icons that control or limit you and put in their place your true self. The template for the script and the introductory remarks to build the emotion are as follows. (In individual counselling the therapist holds his arm out to form a barrier that the client must push through.)

Before beginning, the participant and the therapist come to an agreement in defining the barriers that have been blocking growth. Generally, for the simple cases, there are three barriers: abuser, supporters of abuser, and addictions. For those who have been abused more than once, additional barriers are included.

The candidate stands in the center of the group facing the therapist. The therapist begins by saying the following:

Therapist: Angela, are you ready to break free of all the barriers that hold you back from being the woman you truly want to become?

Angela: Yes, I am ready.

Therapist: Angela, are you ready to walk the painful journey of memories one more time? Are you willing to have your commitment to change challenged by those who do not believe in you and may never support you? Are you strong enough to endure suffering one more time? Are you willing to risk failure and humiliation to become the person you want to be?

Angela: Yes, I want to do it.

Therapist: Angela, are you ready to break through those barriers you worked so hard to confront?

Angela: Yes, I am.

Therapist:	Is there anyone here who wishes to offer support for Angela in her efforts to break free of the chains that hold her? All who wish to support Angela, stand behind her.

After the supporters gather behind Angela, they are instructed as follows:

Therapist:	If you support Angela, as a symbol of that support, place your hand on her back to let her know that you are here for her. [Each place one hand on Angela's back.]
Therapist:	[To the group members standing behind Angela] Now give voice to your support for her.
Various group members:	Angela, you didn't deserve that abuse. You are a good person and you need to go forward with your life. It wasn't your fault. You are a strong and courageous woman.
Therapist:	Angela, even though you have strong support for your journey to break free, you must make the journey alone. There are a number of barriers you must break through to find freedom. The barriers will now be constructed for you.

Angela turns around to face the women who supported her. They form a gauntlet of four pairs of women, with each pair facing Angela, hands joined to form the symbolic barriers.

Barrier 1: The Abuser

Barrier one is always the primary and generally the most frightening abuser. It is often the father, stepfather, or rapist. The candidate has done this difficult role play earlier in the program, and this is the reprise. The candidate is stronger now. She knows what to say and is able to practice her new philosophy. Sexual abuse is wrong. What happened to her was wrong. What happened resulted in problems that she has worked hard to overcome. They will now be addressed again. She is now well on her way on this journey to more fully resolve and then leave behind these issues. In all of life's unfairness, the issues are hers to conquer one more time.

Therapist:	Angela, approach the first barrier. This is the barrier that represents your uncle and father who abused you.
Barrier One:	[The therapist stands beside the two women who face Angela and join hands to form a barrier. The therapist, speaking for the barrier, says:] We represent your uncle and father who abused you. We speak for them. We want you to keep the abuse quiet. We want your silence to protect the family, to keep shame from being spread to the family. We want you to carry the shame of the abuse forever. We value secrecy more than your healing. We want you to take responsibility for the abuse, even though you were only little; we'd like it better that way.
	Angela faces the barrier and responds:
Angela:	It wasn't my fault; I'm breaking free of the hold you have on me. I refuse to carry that shame anymore. That shame is yours.
	Then Angela physically pushes through the joined hands of the first barrier.

Barrier 2: Indirect Abuse

Barrier two is often, but not always, a person from the abusive experience who did not directly abuse the victim but who failed to take action to prevent the continuation of the abuse. Often this person is the mother in the dysfunctional home. The child was convinced the mother knew about the abuse because, from the child's perspective, the pain and agony experienced were obvious in every expression, he or she made, even if it was not directly stated. Often the mother in this situation has been abused herself and she lives her life encapsulated within well-practised errors in thinking that arise from abuse: rationalization, denial, and minimization. Often, she does not know at a conscious level that her child has also been abused. She has lived a lifetime minimizing the impact of her own abuse. How could she accept, understand and cope with the abuse of her child when she could not speak of her own abuse?

Therapist:	Angela, approach the second barrier (formed by two women). This is the barrier that represents your mother who never supported you.
Barrier Two:	[The therapist, speaking for the barrier says:] I am the mother who didn't support you. I want you to minimize the abuse; I want you to pretend it wasn't a big deal, that it was less than it was. I want you to pretend that it didn't hurt that much. If you could keep pretending it didn't hurt, it would make it easier for me, your mother, to not do anything about it—easier for me to live with my own inadequacy if you just keep quiet.
Angela:	Mom, I'm not pretending it didn't hurt—it was horrible, and I've struggled with it ever since. It has haunted me and interfered with me being the women I want to be. I'm living in the truth now. It did hurt, and I am dealing with it.

Barrier Two:	As your mom, I may have to ban you from the family. I might not talk to you anymore. It's too hard for me to face; I am too ashamed. I have never dealt with my own abuse, so I can't deal with yours.
Angela:	I have to take responsibility for solving my own problems. If you can't deal with the abuse in our family, the abuse that happened to me, that's your problem. I'm dealing with it. I'm breaking through this barrier that's holding me back.

Angela pushes through the barrier.

Barrier 3: Other Forms of Abuse

Generally, some other abuse has been perpetrated upon the client after the initial abuse. Victims of sexual abuse, for example, often go on to live in an environment where other forms of abuse are imminent. As well, the victims of abuse often select partners who are abusive, as this type of relationship, with its blend of love and disrespect, feels familiar. For this generic example, we will presume that Angela lived with domestic violence in her relationship.

Therapist:	Angela, please approach the third barrier. This is the barrier that represents your abusive partner.
Barrier Three:	[The therapist speaks for the barrier:] I represent the husband who physically abused you. I want you to remember that no one else will want you. You have to stay in this abusive relationship. It's the best you will ever do. I only hit you when you deserve it, when you make me mad.

Angela: I refuse to be in a relationship with you. I didn't deserve to be beaten by you, and I will not put up with it anymore. You are an abusive and insecure person, and I refuse to be in a relationship with you. I deserve a relationship where I'm respected. I'll be alone before I will be with you.

Angela breaks through this barrier.

Barrier 4: Alcohol and Drug Excesses

This is the barrier of alcohol and drug excesses that served as a means of coping with abuse.

Therapist: Angela, now approach barrier four. This barrier represents how you cope with your abuse by softening it and not facing it, by drinking and using drugs.

Barrier Four: [The therapist speaks for the barrier:] Angela, we are your friends who love you. We want you to party with us. We want you to drown your pain with alcohol and soften your suffering with drugs. We want you to be like us: be a person who covers up her pain and suffering with partying, drugs, and alcohol. Please be with us and love us. We love you, especially when you're drunk.

Angela: I am leaving alcohol and drugs behind. I only used them to hide from my problems. I used them to try to pretend that what happened didn't bother me, but it did. I want to quit alcohol and drugs and deal with life directly, no matter how hard it is.

After the candidate has broken through the last barrier, the therapist draws the exercise to a close with a conclusion such as this.

Therapist: Angela, you have now broken through the barriers that prevent you from reaching your full potential. Your efforts today symbolize your courage to confront those who have hurt you. You have freed yourself of the restrictions, the chains that hold you back. You are free to be the best person you can be. Congratulations! Please accept the congratulations of the others in the group.

      Then the other participants usually hug the successful candidate and group conversation follows.

The Breaking Free exercise often has a stilted and artificial feel. Nevertheless, I believe that it presents an historical series of life events in symbolic form that the client can address and resolve from both a cognitive and emotional perspective.

I have used this exercise in individual counselling with me as the therapist having the client push my blocking arm out of the way to symbolize breaking through the barriers. I believe however, the exercise is much more powerful and effective in the group format.

The client is now ready for the last exercise in the program: My Journey So Far.

CHAPTER 16

Step Seven: My Journey So Far

Once you have immersed yourself in this program, you become committed to completing all of the exercises, as completion represents not only a personal accomplishment but a social measure of success as judged by the other group members. In the My Journey So Far exercise you speak to the group about your healing journey. In this exercise you are often speaking, from written material that you have prepared, to your therapists and fellow group members who have come to know you and your journey. You know that they appreciate and respect you and that they have witnessed your efforts to overcome extremely difficult historical issues. They admire you and look forward to your summarizing and concluding comments, which form the focus of this exercise.

Most people have written something in preparation. Many begin with reflections on their initial fears and anxieties:

> When I started here, I saw other women having the courage to face their issues. I did not believe I could be that brave—then it began for me, too! I knew that it was important for me to share what happened.

When you reach this point you are able to tell your story from a perspective much different than the one you held upon entering the program. This exercise allows you to affirm and consolidate the gains that you have made, to reflect upon your progress to date, and to set a direction for your journey beyond the Icons of the past. Now you are able to look at your life as a journey where you are moving forward, where you feel more in control of your course and more confident about the new direction you are taking. In this effort, when it is done well, you will explain to yourself and others the impact traumatic experiences have had upon your life. You will have connected past traumas endured to bad choices made later. In your speech, you may express that you now understand, accept, and forgive your self-sacrifice, your self-condemnation, and your self-indulgence. Your words will quite possibly reveal feelings of being refreshed, renewed, and reborn. You might choose to explain that the journey forward to the future had to begin by first turning inward, to face the confusion of your inner compass. Your inner life was a place where historical figures, the Icons, were living. They were sending alarming warnings, sirens of caution, and images of past pain that you needed to address with others as your witnesses. Until now, these painful Icons were lodged in a place that prevented personal growth.

When you reach the final stages, you will be able to speak about how this therapeutic approach allowed you to shut down the Icons, bringing peacefulness and resolution to your inner life. In speaking about your journey to healing, you may reflect upon finding a sense of clarity and self-control that you had not previously known. When you comment upon the overall perspective that this allows, you will be able to report that your troubled history has moved farther into the past—a past you can turn to when you choose, not a past that has its own energy to control you, distract you, and draw you back. You will speak about how it feels to be free. Here is an example of one woman's efforts at completing her Journey So Far exercise:

My Journey So Far—A Road to a Better Me!

When I entered the program, I was really in a bad place mentally and emotionally. My problems go back to when

I was young. It started when I was about 12 years old; my virginity was taken by force. My older sister's friend took me out to a bar where someone gave me a date-rape drug. My voice and my body were paralyzed; I could not scream nor move. I could feel the pain though, and I knew what was happening. The police found me in a pool of vomit and blood. They took me to the hospital, where they [tested me with] a rape kit, videotaped a statement, and called my mom.

This horrible incident would have been easier to deal with if I would have had some family support. At the time, my mom was just in the beginning of court hearings from when she was raped and assaulted ... She never asked if I was okay or talked to me about what happened. It seemed like she was oblivious and did not care. I felt worthless, dirty, and bad. I felt like nobody gave a shit, so why should I?

I started using meth, skipping school, and running away from home. I was pulled into a life of crime. I started stealing, selling drugs, and committing fraud. I was essentially numb. I had no feelings of good or bad. I did not give a shit about anything or anyone, because no one gave a shit about me. All my boyfriends were abusive, and I thought that was the best I could do, that that was all I was worth. I was in and out of jail, and the only time I was ever sober was when I was locked up. I have a son who is partly retarded from a man who tried to kill me on more than one occasion during my pregnancy.

Since I was raped as a little girl, I have been abusing myself constantly. Since I started the Courage of Women program, I learned a lot about myself. I discovered that the way I was feeling and thinking about myself is how most who are assaulted think. For me, that meant I was not alone; for the first time, someone actually cared enough to listen to what I had to say. I found out that I was not a bad person; I just had some bad things happen to me. Being in the group has taught me to think and feel differently. I know now that I was not to blame, and I have nothing to be ashamed of or hide.

At first I did not want to talk about it, I was scared what people were going to think about me, but the people who run the group were amazing, and the other group members were so supportive. It was as if a weight had just been lifted off my shoulders once I realized that I was not going to be judged or ridiculed. I was able to disclose about all the abuse I have been through in my life. I think the biggest turning point was when I did a role play with Dr. Pugh. It was tough and really scary. At first, I felt all the rage and hatred I had inside of me come to the surface. It was hard to talk without crying; there were so many things I wanted to say, but I just could not find the words. Finally, I just let it all out—all of what I wanted them to hear. They helped me open the door, and all the pain and hurt that I had been through came out. In the role plays, I was able to tell the people who hurt me about how they had made my life a prison. After the role plays, I felt more alive than I had in a really long time.

The next thing I did in the group was the Cloak of Shame exercise. This one really got me thinking. It made me not want to carry my shameful guilt bag around anymore, that I no longer had to. I made myself a promise when I was stomping on that cloak; I promised away all my shame and guilt.

I finally have everything out in the open. I have had my pain heard and acknowledged. I have had people know and understand what I have been through. I know now that there are people who believe my story and believe in me. I am finally free. I carried my bag of shame for over 14 years. I used drugs like meth to try to hide that bag from myself and others, committed crimes so that I could get the drugs to hide the bag; it was like a never-ending circle. Going through the steps in the program with the support of the other group members, who were always there to listen, was life-changing.

The Courage of Women group has freed my spirit and my soul. Now I am confident that as I embark on my new journey in life I will never feel the need to stuff away that shameful guilt. The shame and the guilt are gone, and in their place lies the courage and confidence of a survivor. That's me, a survivor. I have a long way to go to be complete, since I still have an addiction to beat, but now I no longer have an excuse to use. For the first time, I actually feel like I can beat it, as if I deserve to beat it. I want to use my experience to help others to help themselves, so I will always be willing to be the shoulder for someone to cry on. For those of you who have not yet begun to overcome the obstacles that lie ahead, I encourage you to try. The Courage of Women group, I believe, has exactly what we need to heal; just give it a chance. The program has given me a voice that I am no longer ashamed or scared to use. To the director of this center, if there was ever one request, it would be that more of the women who start this group be given the opportunity to work through all seven steps. I firmly believe that I have been given the opportunity of a lifetime having been able to complete all the steps in this group. ... I want to feel things other than shame and guilt. I know the road in front of me will not be easy, and there's still gonna be times when I am not going to feel so confident, but I know in my heart that I don't have to be ashamed of who I am. I am a woman with the courage to change.

CHAPTER 17
My Personal Journey

With my years of striving to be an objective thinker, I realize that I should not be personal in the explanation of this theory. However, when developing this program and witnessing its successes, I thought I should try some of these exercises myself. The exercises were developed out of my experiences in therapy, out of trial and error, and out of research into certain types of treatment. Psychodrama had always been an interest of mine and I believed in the impact of the powerful role play. I developed the skills to play the adversary in a therapeutic fashion, a technique that few others used in the manner that I had developed. But I had never done the role plays applying my own problems to them and using another psychologist to play the adversary.

Then it struck me. How could I ask others to do these difficult role plays if I had never done them myself? I fell into the defensive strategy used by most of my clients. I said to myself the words that you might say too: "I've worked through that issue. I don't need to do the role play. Look how good my life is now; that's proof I have resolved all my issues."

Still, I felt that was less than the truth. I heard a little voice say, "What about your own logic: if you have worked it out, the role play won't hurt anything?" Being a fair-minded person, a philosophy I sincerely try to cling to, I knew that there was no honest way to avoid the effort. However, I could feel a stubborn resistance. Every time I contemplated doing it, something inside would encourage resistance. I was just the same as every client I had counselled! My resistance to these exercises, especially taking on the role play, was strong. I fought through it.

"What is the first Icon within you, George Pugh that should be addressed? Be honest. Put it out there, just as you ask of every client you face. Say it."

Initial Role Play

Mine was the problem of my father and his excessive drinking. I had told others about it, but not in any detail and not with the admission of the resignation I felt. I never confronted him about it. Like most of my clients, I had initially been too little and always too uneasy to confront the father I loved so much. Even when I was a man, when my father got drunk on my mother's 70th birthday, I did not confront him. I was embarrassed by his conduct. My mother was as well. We had family visiting to celebrate and nobody said anything. What kind of man was I? Many of my male clients had assaulted their fathers for abusing their mothers. Their solutions had been too extreme, but I could not even say the words at the time.

My father is now no longer with us. It's too late to confront him directly. Nevertheless, according to the theory, I should do it. The Icon should be shut down. Was I really carrying that Iconic echo: "Keep quiet; be a good boy; don't confront Daddy"? Was I carrying the generalization of that to other male authority figures: "Don't confront your boss or any male authority figure"? I could think of many examples when I did take a stand, but did I take that stand with a little extra aggression to get over the fear that I carried for my father? Possibly.

I arranged for an excellent psychologist to take me on and do the role play. It was my wife. She was up for it. I must admit, I struggled within. The voice, that Iconic reaction, said, "Don't do it—it won't feel right to do the role play." But I forced myself. When I did it, I said all those things that should have been said. As best I recall, it went something like this, with the remarks offered by my wife, in the role of my father, included as part of the dialogue.

Father: Son, I understand you want to talk with me. I'm ready to listen and talk.

GP: Dad, I was always very disappointed in you when you were drinking so much. It was very upsetting for me.

Father: I didn't know that.

GP: There was one time, at Christmas; you were so drunk you couldn't cut the turkey. It made it a very sad time for me. I worried about Mom. I could tell she was upset. I was only 12 or 13.

Father: I never knew you felt that way.

GP: I remember the time you got drunk on Mom's 70th birthday; your sisters were there. It was like you were a little child. You were so drunk you could hardly talk. It was embarrassing and then the next day, nothing was said. It was like it never happened. Or, if it did happen, it was okay. Well, it wasn't okay, and unfortunately, I wasn't man enough to say anything. I regret that. I felt like a coward.

Father: Well, you've said it now.

GP: Why were you like that?

Father: Well, that's how men were when I was raised. That was the way to be. In my early years, drinking was just part of being a man. I drank with my dad and my uncles. That's just how we related. They were my role models—many of them had problems. I'm not blaming them. I'm just saying that's how it was. I want to say to you son, "I'm sorry. It was wrong. I hope you can forgive me."

GP: Oh, Dad. I always loved you. Forgiving is not an issue with me. It's just that I had to say these things to get it right—even if it is a little late.

Father: I'm glad we had this talk. I always loved you.

I had done it. In retrospect I realized that an anxiety hurdle had been in the way. I just had to jump over to get to the conversation. Then, in the days that followed, I noticed that the inner feeling of resentment for my father had left me, or at least it was somehow different. I just felt more relaxed about it. As well, I experienced a deeper feeling of forgiveness for him. I had always thought of him as a good man who had his problems, but now I felt a greater understanding. As well, my sense of being a coward within had left me.

Once I got into it, the role play was easy to do. Words, of course, come easy for me. I let the success of the role play percolate in my mind as I continued with this book and continued with the Courage of Women program and with my private clients. I became more passionate about the program, because the basic principle had been, if not proven, at least supported with my own experience. Here I was, a relatively successful man, dragging that problem around and really achieving what successes I had managed in spite of that issue. I now took the position not only from a theoretical but also from a personal view point that any problem, big or small, for women and men, could be addressed in this fashion and lead to, at a minimum, steps towards a sense of inner peace.

I truly believe that I am no different than others regarding issues of this nature. All of my clients have similar issues. I am sure that most have suffered greater abuse. My father never struck my mother or his children; he seldom yelled and he always treated us with respect, even when he was drinking. He was just embarrassing. In his best moments, during a family crisis, he was our champion. So I know that others had it a lot worse than I did. If they could take on my strategies, they too would find an inner sense of resolution and peace.

Then I tried a role play with my mother. I have written about mothers as being the source of so much misery for their children. You may think I really do not care for mothers and that my mother must not have been the best, but she was. She was an angel, really. I always felt loved by her. I always felt special. I was the firstborn. I truly thought that gave me a special status. Nevertheless, she did leave me out of her will. I know it was because she thought I was well-to-do and not in need of any of her inheritance, but to be honest, it was hurtful. To be left a lot less than my siblings did not seem right. So I role played that issue and again I experienced a deeper sense of forgiveness and letting go

The next major Icon for me—and I am afraid again to say it—was with God. I knew I carried shame, guilt, and frustration regarding what I had been told about the nature of God, how I was required to think about him as a child, and how I thought about him when an adult. I believed that God-related guilt and shame still lingered unnecessarily within. I completed the role play and felt a sense of relief, resolution, and inner peace. In my first draft of this book, I had included the dialogue of the role play. However, after reading it many times in the editing stage, I feared that it might be interpreted as proselytizing my religious philosophy. This was clearly not my intent. I did not want to distract from the primary theme of the book, so for that reason, and on the advice of a respected editor, I removed the content of that role play.

In essence, the role play with God fits within the same dynamic as any other relationship that may have abusive qualities. If the explanation or teaching of your God has presented Him in an abusive and harsh light, and you have experienced excessive guilt, shame, and anger as a consequence, then possibly a role play would be helpful. I recall one client whom I helped with this issue. She was angry at God for the death of her mother. The role play allowed for the expression of this anger, reconciliation with the spiritual side of life, and a gentler and more understanding perception of her God.

If you are struggling in your relationship with the spiritual side of life and would like to read the dialogue from my role play regarding this issue, you can contact me through my web page, and I will consider releasing it at that time.

Six Months Later

I re-read my personal role play with God six months later and realized, at that time, that I felt a greater sense of inner integrity, a sense that I had resolved my issue – of living in fear that I would be judged and would come up short. Now, I believe I am in that place where I will judge my own effort from a gentler, more understanding and personal perspective. Possibly, I could have spoken with a preacher or minister about these religious issues and that might have worked, but, to be honest, I had tried that without satisfaction. Somehow, talking directly was effective for me.

I was speaking about that role play with God with a good friend who is a very spiritual man. He listened and asked, "Where is God in your life now?" I hadn't thought about that, but in the next moment, an image of God flashed across my mind. He was sitting in the back of a theatre, next to my mother and father, watching me on the stage of life. They were happy there as they watched my life going forward without any interference. The Icons had found peace too.

That's it. That's the end of my journey of carrying the Icons of the past. Now, I go forward without that burden, just as I promised in my treatment programs. I now feel freer to rise to the challenges that life brings without the haunting reminders of past survival strategies that prevented and inhibited a full effort.

That is what I want for you.

CHAPTER 18
Personal Development Is a Lifelong Journey and Struggle

Is there hope for you? Do you feel your life has been ruined by the injustice you suffered as a child, youth, or adult? My mind goes back to the young woman who related the following to me:

> *I've been a victim of abuse as long as I can remember. I built walls up that I never wanted to come down. This program reached far down into my heart and hit the very foundation on which I built those walls. Those walls came crashing down. Through the steps in this program and the encouragement of the psychologists, I worked through the pain and trauma. My spirit has come back. I now have a voice.*

That woman was convinced that she could never have a full life, that her life was ruined. She did all of the exercises in this book. She struggled with them. I saw joy on her face. I witnessed as she slowly took control of her own life. She found healing, and so can you.

I vividly recall speaking with a woman in her 80s. She told me of this burden she was carrying. It was anxiety described as heaviness on her chest. When I recorded her history, she told me of a time when she was four years old. The family was poor. At Christmas her mother managed to give her older brothers and sisters Christmas gifts. There was none for her. She was told, "You can have the wrapping paper."

This lady carried that moment as a lifelong symbol of her mother's rejection. She was convinced that her mother did not love her and, further, had intentionally humiliated and hurt her. She was convinced that her mother had ruined her life. This was the Iconic dynamic that limited her.

Following my encouraging and supportive explanation of the purpose and power of the role play, she agreed, after significant resistance, to give it a try. I played the part of the mother, returned from the other side. I heard her say the truth to her mother: "You were horrible to me"; "You never loved me"; "How could you do that to me?" I, as the mother, explained that I, too, had suffered abuse; that I too had been damaged. I told her that, as a consequence of suffering, I was unable to release the love she deserved. My client refused to listen. She could not let go of the life denied her, of the abuse and neglect that defined her. For 75 years she had reviewed in her mind over and over that story of the wrapping paper. The Christmas holidays became a yearly reminder of her mother's coldness. Wrapping paper took her back to that powerful moment of rejection. The die was cast and it held in spite of all my efforts.

She had finally spoken the horrible truth in the role play and revealed its lifetime of condemnation. At the end of the session, she insisted that no healing had occurred. She was angry at me. She refused any insight that I, in the role of mother, had suggested. After we broke from the role play, I explained to her that she had made great progress. She discounted my conclusion. She clung to her resentment. I encouraged her to let it go. She refused. I explained that if she remained determined to live the remainder of her life filled with resentment; she would find it difficult to release her love for her children, grandchildren, and great-grandchildren. She was surprised and upset with the conclusion that she had become a milder version of her rejecting mother.

She clung to the only justice she had known: her previously secret condemnation of her mother's betrayal. She was right. It was not fair. From my perspective, she was halfway home, but she could go no farther. That little piece of justice, her right to hate her mother, was all she had left. It appeared she would never release it. As a result, not only was she denied a life without the love of a mother, she was destined to live a life with a heavy heart, where her own children and their children were experiencing her as alienated and bitter.

When I first wrote the above paragraphs, I had assumed that I had failed this woman. I presumed she would never return. She left the one session commenting on her disappointment in me and my approach, still clinging to her resentment. I had presumed that her refusal to accept any insight was her own condemnation, but I was wrong. One year later, she returned. She seemed happier; her eyes were brighter. She told me that whatever it was that we had done, it had worked. The heaviness in her chest was gone. I could feel that her energy was more positive.

From this experience I learned more about the nature of resistance. Often the client clings to old ways of thinking; in this case, to the concept of the mother as an evil person. Even when the role play is resisted before it begins ("I don't think that will work"), and resisted during its execution ("This isn't working—my mother would never say that") and following its completion ("I still feel the same—it didn't work"), success may still result, and the resentment will leave. Once you do the role play, you break the hold of the Icon, and your concept of the historical problem begins to change to a more realistic perspective. Sometimes it just takes time to process what occurred in the role play.

I have had many successes with Iconic therapy. The primary requirements are disclosure and role play. The remaining exercises will consolidate your successes and elevate you even further. All you have to do is accept the possibility that this approach might work and then try it.

We are all born into flawed environments. As a consequence, we all suffer at the hands of others, and we are vulnerable to carrying on the cycle of abuse. We may resort, in our confused effort to cope with our own abuse, to hurting those we love. We have to break from that cycle of abuse, where one generation abuses the next, where inflicting pain on the vulnerable is rationalized. We do not have to be part of that energy.

Once you do these exercises, you will find success, even though years of practicing the wrong solution do take their toll. All of us carry Icons that remind us of our rejections much longer than necessary. You can have what that elderly lady finally achieved—and much sooner. You can take control of your mind. That is what I want for you. Do not give in to those Icons that still visit you with destructive messages that lead to a toxic and counterproductive inner life. You are worthy of a full life with a clear mind. You can have it. It is there for you. With the methods I've described in this book, you can reprogram your mind. You can change the way you reflexively think.

The key mechanism is the role play. Every time you do a role play with an Icon within, you will alter that memory trace, and you will change the inner destructive messages emanating from that Icon.

There is hope. Do not be a person diminished in whole or in part by the negative events of your past. As part of your journey in life, you can design your own destiny.

In every journey, there is a birth, a beginning. Then there is the nurturing, the shaping by your forbearers. Then there is a life of your own. This final stage is yours. You are the captain of that ship. Take the helm. Do not be held back by fears of the past. If you are ready, and most of you are, take on the Icons. Take control of your mind. If you have the courage, life is yours for the taking.

Do not be the beaten, anxiety-ridden victim of past abuse. Return to that Icon and fight that last fight. You are an informed person now! Take on the primary responsibilities of personhood and grasp control of your own life. You can become the strong one. Take back what is yours: the essence of your being.

If you want to begin on your own, start by writing about the Icons in your life. Write about the injustice you suffered and how it made you feel. Explore on paper how the injustice continues to impact you today. This can be the first step in your journey. Write the truth. Read it to yourself. See it from that written perspective. Read it out loud in private and hear your own voice say the words that should be said.

Prepare yourself to share what you have written with a therapist. Do not presume that you are the first to have experienced this type of injustice. The therapist has heard it before. It is you you! — who have not heard your words spoken with your voice directed to another. Read what you have written to the therapist. Speak those words again while lifting your eyes from your written words to let your inner voice flow with the words that carry the truth. Then take some time to recover. Take time by yourself. Remind yourself, "I am now living in the truth."

Realize that you have started your own revolution. You are the freedom fighter now. Your freedom was taken from you, and now you will fight to get it back. It will not be an easy fight, but it is one you can win. Prepare for the role play. Begin to practice what should be said to the Icon, that abusive person who lives within. Say the horrible truth about how you feel. Ask the tough questions. You deserve the answers. Ask your therapist to play that part. He or she will do it and if it is difficult for them, ask them to read this book and make the preparations.

Take on that role play. It is the secret portal to another life— your life. The change will be enormous and the remaining exercises will be easy.

Remember, the shame is not yours. It never was!

APPENDIX 1

Comments for Therapists: The Theory and Its Development in the Courage of Women Program

I am writing this appendix for therapists and interested others who want to understand the basic principles of Iconic therapy. Potential clients do not need to understand the principles of Iconic therapy to benefit from the therapeutic exercises. It is like driving a car. You don't have to know how the motor works to drive across town; but if the motor is misfiring, you need someone who knows about motors to help you. However, reading about the process of change may bring a greater understanding of how the personality forms and, more importantly, how it can be modified. With that perspective, you, as a potential client, may feel more open to taking on your therapeutic journey. You are, therefore, invited to read on as well.

The purpose of the theory that underlies Iconic therapy is to offer a simple way to understand the complexities of the human psyche. With an understanding of the energy forces within and an awareness of the strategies through which these forces form and find release, client and therapist can engage in therapeutic exercises that lead to healing and a re-structuring of the personality. This section will review and elaborate upon concepts already presented which will hopefully add clarity for those therapists and counsellors interested in understanding and applying these therapeutic techniques.

The Survival Dynamic: The Energy Forces That Drive the Personality

The primary motivating force for the animal species is to maintain itself, to survive. This includes the human species. This need to survive is the underlying energy source that lives within all of us. Even though seldom noticed (because one's life is seldom threatened) it is the most powerful instinctual need of all. When one's life is threatened, their personality is altered to accommodate and survive the threat and to offer protective strategies for future threats. This is the basic premise underlying Iconic therapy. This instinct to survive is structured in two dimensions.

▶ The basic dynamic: To survive as an individual

All individuals have a basic instinct to survive. When one's life is threatened, they instinctively struggle to live. If drowning, one fights to keep afloat, to get to shore. If threatened with a gun, you are terrified and take action to save yourself. If the threat to one's individual survival is mild but ongoing, they adjust and fine-tune their circumstances, behavior, thought processes and personality to maximize chances for safety and survival. Thus, this instinctual need for survival as a person plays a major role in shaping one's personality, and further, this same instinctual need shapes how one conceptualizes and understands their personality.

▶ The second dynamic: To survive as a species

Second, there is an instinctive need within all of us regarding the survival of our species as a whole. We may not notice when we are actualizing this second instinctive energy force within, this interest in the welfare of others, but it happens all the time. As we mature, we long to connect with another to reproduce, so that our species can continue. When we care for and nurture our children, we are fulfilling this basic survival instinct.

This survival-of-the-species need leads to sociological institutions such as marriage, family, community, and country, which support joint efforts for the expression of this energy and striving. These institutions serve as venues for our longing for membership and connection and support the basic instinct to survive as a species. When these institutions are threatened, we fight in a joint effort for survival. If, for example, it is our country that is threatened, we join with our fellow citizens to fight to maintain the survival of this grouping of our species. As well, and more specifically, the survival-of the species energy finds expression in our efforts to assist others with their journey in life.

The survival of our species is also addressed in Iconic therapy when the client has finally overcome the Icons within. Only then will he or she be sincerely energized to assist others who have experienced similar issues. Sharing strategies for survival and offering wisdom and guidance partially fulfill that second survival longing—to elevate the human condition to a level where the rights and freedoms of each individual, child or adult, are given the highest respect. This includes protecting others from harm, thus enhancing their survival. When all of a person's inner personal Icons have been shut down, then he or she will naturally reach out to assist others in their efforts to experience the freedoms of personhood, the emergence of their true selves, and the fulfillment of their survival strivings.

▶ The personality forms to enhance survival

When our survival is threatened, within one or both of these survival dimensions psychological consequences occur, such that, with low threat we feel anxiety, and with high threat, we feel panic. In all threatening situations, we feel compelled to take action to improve our chances for survival. *Our personalities form in a manner to maximize our chances for survival and to minimize any threat to our existence.*

The personality is also shaped by positive life events. If we experience loving and nurturing parents or powerful positive experiences, then our personalities will be shaped in harmony with nurturing energies and circumstances wherein we adopt positive thoughts of ourselves, such as the following:

> I am loved and lovable, and with this mindset I will view the world and my place in it as a place where I will thrive in my efforts to connect with my true self and with others. I will develop my "self" to find a life filled with passion and connection. My efforts will lead to a sense of personal fulfillment and eventually the betterment of the species, beginning with my children.

These positive and nurturing events serve as the foundation for healthy functioning, and the degree to which a person experiences these in his or her upbringing is the degree to which he or she will have the potential for a healthy personality.

If traumatic events are included in the mixture of stimuli that are visited upon the young person or adult, the personality is also shaped to accommodate these life-altering or life-threatening events. Thus, there is a blending of positive and negative events within one's developmental years that contribute to the shaping and formation of the personality. However, it is only the negative events that threaten or compromise one's survival. These generally have the more powerful impact on the formation of the personality. It is the events perceived as life-threatening that result in the formation of Icons within the personality. These Icons are initially formed to improve chances for survival. However, these same protective Iconic forces later interfere with the healthy risk-taking required to achieve higher levels of development. Eventually these forces interfere with that second area of need, the survival-of-the-species dynamic. It is generally these negative events and their mental representations within the psyche, the Icons, which lead to a sense of inner conflict and serve as the underlying motivation for individuals to attend therapy. It is these Icons, the symbolic representatives of one's traumatic and negative memories and their psychological aftermath that are the focus of Iconic therapy.

The structure of the personality

In this model of the psyche we have *the true self,* which has energy and natural directives to strive: first, to survive personally; and second, to contribute to the survival of the species as a whole.

Then we have the *personality,* the manifestation of the true self in its expression of our survival instincts. The personality forms in response to the survival dynamic, first to protect the true self from harm, second, to actualize and embolden the true self and third to strive to enhance the species. This is done initially by reducing personal threat and then by connecting with and supporting loved ones and family.

The threats to survival may come from flawed caregivers, family members or others who struggle with their own issues. Abusive/ abandoning parents, sexual abusers, and other life-threatening individuals and circumstances perpetrate physical and psychological harm upon an individual and, in so doing, compromise and jeopardize the survival of that person. The mental images and cognitive concepts of these experiences, the Icons, form and trigger powerful survival strategies and actions in response to perceived threats. Later, however, *these same forces over-focus the victim on survival strategies, and in so doing, these Icons eventually limit and prevent personal growth.*

A manifestation of the Icon, the mental symbol of the person or the event that threatened survival is the *Iconic echo,* which is heard as an inner voice. It is the voice and image of the Icon, reminding the *true self* that traumatic, life-threatening events might reoccur. The imagery (including sounds and feelings) associated with the life-threatening events reverberates in the mind of the victim, triggered by even mildly stressful stimuli that remind the individual of the abuse scenario. The Iconic imagery encourages the individual to remain vigilant. This mindset triggers the *Iconic reaction*, the intellectual interpretation of what is occurring and the safest cognitive and behavioral strategies to avoid further victimization.

For example, the victim may feel that he has no choice but to choose to comply with the abuser as a means of survival. In this Iconic reaction victims often adopt the beliefs or series of cognitions that support the theme that they deserved to suffer negative events because they are less worthy than others. This type of response to the life-threatening event may become the underlying cognitive strategy to ensure survival. As a consequence, the condemning voice of the perpetrator is personalized with "I" statements such as "I deserved to suffer that life-threatening, abusive event" or "I was at fault all along," as this is a form of cognitive compliance that initially enhances survival. As well, the injustice of this type of cognition is also considered (a reaction to the Iconic reaction), and seeds of frustration and anger are planted.

These inner thoughts often coalesce around the theme "I'm not good enough for anything but survival. I'm just existing." This type of thought processing discourages healthy risk-taking and encourages the primary focus of the survival-oriented personality to be vigilant, guarding against the return of the abuser or anyone similar to that abuser who might threaten existence. The Iconic echo, ("You're not worthy") and its Iconic reaction ("I'm not worthy"), reverberate in harmony throughout the psyche long after survival has been achieved. Often the inner thoughts (Iconic echoes and cognitive Iconic reactions) gain power and strength through countless mental repetitions. These thoughts may become so overwhelming, and upsetting that, in efforts to reduce this constant bombardment of self-condemnations (and the anxiety attached), these individuals engage in anxiety-reducing but self-defeating actions. For example, they will resist taking on any difficult challenge as they fear that, if they fail, abuse and disrespect will rain down on them again.

Their feelings of vulnerability trigger excessive efforts to maintain safety. In this state of mind, victims of abuse and trauma often engage in behaviors that will temporarily lessen their prolonged and heightened state of anxiety and break them from their ongoing vigilance. They turn to addictions to soften that vigilance and their inner pain, sometimes in extremely self-destructive ways.

The Icon within that condemns an individual was initially attached to their personal instinct to survive. These Icons continue to absorb and express unproductive survival energies long after the life-threatening situations have been resolved. These Icons are often out of control within the psyche and have to be shut down. Once the energy has been taken from the Icons, the victim will know and finally accept that their lives are no longer at risk. A sense of safety, inner peace, and self-acceptance will be experienced and they will find themselves interested in their own personal development as it applies to current and future concerns in their journey forward. This improved position will then allow them to turn more completely to the issues beyond personal survival to pursue, for example, their interests in connection with a partner and the development of family. Finally, they will be able to identify and initiate efforts to alleviate the suffering of others and to be of service to the well-being of our species as a whole.

Reshaping the personality

The primary purpose in Iconic therapy is to attack and remove the negative, out of control and counter-productive Icons within the psyche, which found their place and purpose in initial efforts to enhance survival. In therapy, it is essential to begin with a comprehensive interview that will flush out the currents concerns as well as the hidden Icons. Often, these Icons have been created as a consequence of parental abandonment, abusive experiences (physical, sexual, emotional), and traumatic experiences endured later in life. The interview should bring clarity to, not only the presenting problems but also the underlying nature of the Icons within. Often the presenting concerns and the historical issues are related and the ideal therapeutic solution will involve an attack on these two fronts.

The ultimate purpose of the therapy is challenge the Iconic echo ("You're not good enough") and the Iconic reaction ("I will not take any action that will distract me from my survival efforts. To feel safe, I will sooth my sense of loss with addictions and distractions."). This is done by attaching the Icons directly. Once the out-of-control Icons have been shut down, the energy that supports Iconic reactions and their accompanying cognitive distortions (e.g., "I won't try to succeed because I'm not good enough") will be mitigated or eliminated leaving the client in a much better position to face and overcome the problems of everyday life.

A New Direction

I would like each therapist (or aspiring therapist) reading this text to think about this question: *How are my clients different than the imprisoned women and men upon whom this theory was developed?* When taking this perspective, you will realize that negative Icons live within all clients. No upbringing is perfect, and a negative event can be perceived as traumatic by the fragile personality of the client. When this occurs, the Iconic process is launched. Negative Icons are fixed in place and often have an enduring impact that has limited and restricted the personal growth of the client.

The presence of the Icon and its messages are continually reinforced with survival energies that initially reduced anxiety and increased safety-seeking behavior. When your client offered compliance to an abuser their anxiety was reduced and the message of the Icon was accepted and affirmed: "The abuser is right (compliance); maybe I am a bad person. If I keep him happy (Iconic reaction), maybe he won't hurt me as badly. I feel safer thinking this way."

When this strategy allowed some success at the scene of the trauma and during its aftermath, the client felt safer, and survival strategies were reinforced. However, shame, resentment, and anger began to fester as well. It is the purpose of Iconic therapy to reprogram this process.

It is natural for your clients to resist any effort to change the survival strategies that have been incorporated into their personality. Your clients instinctively cling to the way they have been and they feel (erroneously) that their Iconic reactions continue to be essential elements of their essence and their survival. As well, even though the rationalizations to support survival strategies ("I will hold to the belief that I am not worthy") are no longer necessary, these are so well engrained that the client is often unaware of their power and, concomitantly, their recalcitrant habit to cling to the way they have always been. That is why this type of therapy can be so difficult— because its purpose is to alter survival strategies that at one time were functional.

It reminds me of when I taught my children to swim. Their first thought when in the water seemed to be: "That water can kill me; I don't want to drown." Their primitive swimming strategy was this: "The safest way to manage in the water is to never have my mouth underwater. Ideally, if I can keep my entire head above the surface, it will be the safest." This approach may keep a person from drowning, but he or she will never learn how to swim. When teaching swimming then, one has to begin with teaching how to feel safe in the water. The same is true of therapy; the client must feel safe enough to consider the possibility that new strategies and cognitions are required for healing.

The first step in learning how to swim is learning to set aside that primitive, counterproductive survival instinct (keeping the head above water) and then to feel safe enough to try riskier strategies that will eventually lead to swimming. In therapy or counselling then, the first step is to help the client break the silence and feel safe enough to speak honestly about the past life-threatening or very upsetting event or events that created the Icon. Then, once he or she has survived that break from tradition, the therapist will explain the role play in a manner to indicate not only an acknowledgment of its difficulty but also its power to bring about change. This is the moment where the therapist must be sensitive, acutely aware and respectful of the level of resistance of the client. It is in this moment that the client will be torn between going into fight modality or retreating to flight and choosing to avoid dealing directly with the core issue.

In general, the difficulties with implementing this type of therapy must be addressed by establishing for the client feelings of safety and acceptance. When they realize that their safety and integrity are not at risk in the therapeutic setting, they will move forward. There are times when a staged or graduated approach is best. Often you will find that you, as the therapist, will be able to have the client agree that if he or she could complete the role play, it would be a good thing, but for the moment they cannot do it. Once you reach this point, then you have made significant progress and generally the client will take on the role play in the next session. As the therapist you might say the following:

Therapist: A role play with your mother would be an excellent therapeutic exercise. It would finally allow the release of the toxic emotions you have held for so long.

The client: I don't think I'm ready for that.

Therapist: I hear you. It is a challenging and possibly difficult exercise. But it does have a very therapeutic impact. Here is a way to think about it that might make it less threatening for you. Try thinking about it this way. It would merely be an exercise where we would be saying words to each other. No one else will hear. It is just you and me in this room saying things to each other. The door is closed. Your mother will never know what has been said, unless you tell her. I say nothing to anyone about what is said. It is all confidential.

The client: If you think of it that way it is not so bad.

Therapist:	Nevertheless, maybe today is not the day to do it. Here is another way to think about it. If you were able to do it – would it be a good thing to have done?
The client:	Maybe, Yes, I think it might be a good thing.
Therapist:	How about we agree that you will think about doing it on another occasion. But definitely, we won't do it today. Another day – maybe?
Client:	Sure, I will think about it.

The turning point in Iconic therapy is the role play. Once the client takes on the first role play then they are much more open to take on the remaining role plays that will release the toxic emotions that still remain lodged in place.

Once the client feels safe enough to confront the Icon in this new modality, the pace of therapy begins to accelerate. When he or she finally enters the role play an actualization of assertive, emotionally honest, deeply personal behaviors will manifest albeit with an awkwardness and uncomfortableness. With this effort the client finally discovers that they will not die in their effort to assert their sense of truth and their longing for justice. Finally the truth is spoken and they learn that their personality has not been destroyed by their efforts in the role play but enhanced and strengthened. They are taking the first steps to live and thrive in a place apart from the abusive mental environment that has encapsulated them. In this moment they are finally living in opposition to and apart from the controlling and life-threatening memories. They have taken the first steps towards integrity, emotional honesty and freedom.

▶ Therapists: Consider addressing your own issues, even if they are minor

Some of the earlier chapters in this book may have triggered deep, upsetting emotions. If that has happened to you, even if you are an experienced therapist, it is a signal from within of a yearning to release these long-repressed feelings of anxiety, fear, anger, and shame. These feelings will get in the way of your efforts to actualize your true self, and they will prevent you from helping your clients with issues that remind you of your own unresolved concerns. Ideally, all of us should address the limiting Icons within. As a therapist, you should take part in an Iconic workshop and address your own concerns. This will serve two purposes. First, it will familiarize you with the principles of Iconic therapy from the view point of the client. Second, it will take you to a higher level of personal integration and maturity. This will lead to a clearer understanding of what is required from you in your therapeutic relationship with your clients.

▶ The therapist's mission

It is your mission as a therapist to help set the agenda for your clients. It is your job to help them find the field of battle, that place where the Icons live, sapping energy and discouraging focus for anything beyond mere survival. You need to prepare them, if they are willing, for therapy that will challenge and possibly upset them. From a therapist's perspective you will see more clearly the devastating impact of the Icons within as your clients are often blinded by shame, secrecy, errors in thinking, cognitive distortions and counterproductive resistance that bind outdated survival strategies to discouragement and hopelessness. It is for you to help them comprehend the nature of the Icons that limit them in many aspects of their functioning. It is up to you to persuade your client to believe that the battle against the Icons is one they can win if and when they find the courage to take on this challenge.

▶ Building Trust within the Therapeutic Relationship

It is difficult for the therapist to establish for each client a belief in the therapeutic exercises designed to guide and structure their efforts. As therapists, each of us needs to secure a sense of trust with our clients, so that they will believe that their efforts will lead to something beneficial: release and resolution from their lingering anxiety, shame, anger and continual self-condemnation.

We, the therapists, must understand that our role has to be delivered with a precise sense of tone, sensitivity, and caring. We have to set aside any energy within us that considers our own goals more important than our respect for the client. The client's right to refuse these very difficult therapeutic tasks, whether stated or implied, has to be honored and respected.

You will begin to understand your client's resistance as a naturally occurring survival-related phenomenon. Their continued efforts to protect themselves from any threat of future abuse or disrespect have had a devastating side effect. They have carried within them a vortex of unexpressed and sometimes frightening emotions, including anxiety, shame, and fear of embarrassment. These emotions kept them safe and hyper-alert in the aftermath of trauma. In the present, however, these same emotions are being triggered by the stressors of daily life. As a consequence, these clients have continued to cling to their early survival strategies—which include experiencing self-demeaning Iconic echoes that remind them that they are inadequate and align them with the same feelings they experienced following the hurtful events of the past. They are continually reminded by their own thoughts, that somehow they deserved to be mistreated and that it was in their best interest to remain secretive about what they had endured.

When they meet with their therapist, these same survival strategies will be triggered by some of the discussions in the early phases of therapy. Two objectives need to be addressed simultaneously: respecting and understanding the client's survival-oriented resistance to taking on the healing journey; while, at the same time, clarifying and championing the nature and benefits of the healing journey with you as their guide. Clients will always be torn. They want to break free, but they fear failure, shaming, and humiliation. Their burden will be your burden. When they can trust you enough they will let you carry the guiding light and then they will move forward.

After establishing the trust relationship, breaking through the resistance to sharing the nature of the abuses becomes the first objective in therapy, and with good technique the first breakthrough will be the disclosure. However, the client's resistance to releasing repressed emotions by speaking directly to the Icon in the role play is much more powerful and requires a highly skilled therapist to lead the way. The client will often resist, even though they know that these toxic emotions continue to leach into every aspect of their lives.

It is very important to never force disclosure or force participation in any of the exercises that follow the disclosure. The resistance of the client, even though it may appear counterproductive, must be respected. This is very important. Any coercive effort, no matter what the intent, is in itself abusive. This should be explained to all who participate in an Iconic treatment approach.

> We will never force you to do anything. Being forced to do something is what happened when you were mistreated—you were forced to do or take part in something that should never have happened. We, in our efforts to assist you on your healing journey, do not want to be part of anything coercive. We will be encouraging you to complete exercises that will be difficult but the final choice will always be yours.

Forcing someone against their will only repeats, in effect, the abuse scenario. Even taking part in a process where we coerce another person to think in a certain way is abusive. This is the very opposite of what we want to accomplish. We want our clients to take charge of their own lives, by making their own choices and, after consulting with us, symbolically confront those who have taken their power and silenced their voice. As therapists, we want to be allies in their fight to take control of their minds and the Iconic echoes within.

There will be times when you, as a therapist, may be apprehensive regarding the emotionally charged nature of the role play. For example, there were moments, although quite rare, when I knew that if the client were to enter a state of rage, they could possibly lose control and hurt me. However, I also knew that together we had formed a therapeutic alliance that carried with it their concern for me and that they not lose control. Even in these situations I would carry on with the role play with strategies I knew would work. I knew that the control mechanism within the client, next to the anger, would allow them to complete this exercise in a safe fashion. I encouraged them to remember, even when the extreme anger came to them, that this was an exercise in which they would remain in control of their anger, so that it could be released in words and not violence. Anger of this intensity has to find an acceptable modality for release to allow for a return of peace and resolution within. **It is essential that the anger is delivered, in feelings shaped with words that are directed toward the Icon.** Getting angry at the wrong person in an overly aggressive or violent way obviously did not work; the inmates I had worked with had already done that many times. The anger had to be expressed verbally and directly to the Icon in the role-play format. As the therapist, here is how I would explain it to extremely angry clients:

> I understand and accept that your anger is extreme. If what happened to you had happened to me I, too, would be extremely angry. Now, try to think of it this way. That anger now pervades your whole life. It is released in many situations inappropriately, sometimes through violence. That is the anger you soften and avoid with the use of drugs and alcohol. You know that anger prevents you from being a good mother and a good wife (or a good father and a good husband). It will prevent you from being the person you want to be. As part of your healing journey, it is very important that

your anger finds the right form of expression to allow its release. If it remains within you, it may destroy you, and others, too.

It is appropriate to point out at this juncture that the discussion of excessive anger with a client in a prison situation is not unique to that setting. This same situation occurs with clients from every walk of life who have been attending a psychologist or counsellor in the community with their "anger management" or "temper control" problem. In most cases, there is that early traumatic experience, or experience of unfairness, that remains unresolved. The same treatment approach will work in the community setting with individual or group counselling, as well as it did in the prison program.

▶ The power of group therapy

The Iconic process can be applied within individual counselling sessions. However, the group process exponentially accelerates and enhances the potential for change. Once a victim of trauma learns that they are not alone with their suffering, that there are others just like them, their perception of their place in the world begins to change. That secret, penetrating error in thinking—"I have been singled out for suffering because I am truly unworthy"—is challenged with their first attendance in the group-therapy situation. Once they observe others disclosing, their willingness to let down their guard, to break from years of secrecy, and to risk shaming is strengthened. The potential for healing increases within the dynamics of the group process. I urge therapists, especially those of you who are working in institutions, to take on the challenge of running a group-therapy program and use the Iconic approach. Your impact will be multiplied tenfold, and the number of clients you help will be increased significantly.

With the group-therapy approach, you will observe that when other group members lead the way, beginning participants are emboldened to take on the extremely difficult role play. An awakening of insight will occur for those beginning their healing journey after they witness the suffering, and then victory, of someone else's successful role play. When they observe others who also harbor out-of-control destructive emotions, release these potentially soul-destroying forces in this setting, they know that they can find resolution as well. They realize that they have finally come to a place where there is heightened potential for change. Finally there is hope.

After some of the group complete the first two exercises, Disclosure and Role Play, a critical mass of therapeutic energy will form that will touch and nurture the remaining participants. The group will begin to live in a new place:

- a place of emotional release and recovery
- a place of sanctuary and healing
- a place where reintegration and transformation occurs
- a place where defensiveness is reduced and openness and self-acceptance blossom

Comments for therapists: How to do the difficult role play

The role play, with the therapist playing the part of the adversary, is the primary therapeutic intervention that separates Iconic therapy from most other forms of therapy.

Beginning psychologists, psychiatrist, counsellors, and therapists sometimes struggle when they consider taking part in the role play and playing the part of the Icon. Many therapists and caregivers do not receive training for this type of therapy, and further, the therapeutic interventions recommended here are unique and have been developed specifically with regard to the principles involved in the Iconic approach. Do not let uneasiness or shyness with role-playing the perpetrator of abuse get in the way of your participation in this very powerful therapeutic technique. Set aside your inhibitions, and allow yourself to be an important part in the healthy transitions that will unfold with these therapeutic efforts.

Playing the part of the abandoning parent, sexual perpetrator, physical abuser, or murderer is not as difficult or as awkward as it may first appear. However, in these therapeutic interventions it is very important to play the role properly, as it will allow clients to release their contained and guarded emotions and find their true voice. There are a number of cautions to adhere to when taking on this therapeutic intervention. First, there is a tendency, almost a longing, on the part of the psychologist or counsellor to play the Icon as too powerful for the client. The novice therapist tends to conceptualize and actualize the Icon as extremely evil and extremely frightening. They presume that they should play the role accurately with this concept in mind. The novice therapist might, for example, portray the Icon as an irrational, rigid, and condemning entity with excellent verbal skills—an evil person who can deny or minimize whatever occurred. **A word to therapists—do not portray the Icon in this manner!** It can be counter-therapeutic to role-play the Icon as too negative or recalcitrant.

Both therapist and client need to remember that the purpose of the exercise is to present a safe situation where the client will be able to release their anger and repressed feelings for injustices suffered, in a setting where the client's efforts will not be shut down. The client will find some closure by placing her or his anger, shame, and sadness into the vessel provided, the psychologist or counsellor playing the part of the Icon. Therapists, remember that your client has been victimized for an extended period—first by the event itself, next by the Icon formed as a result, and then by the Iconic echo that continues to resonate within. Remember that the reason the client could not work through the issue with the perpetrator is that the perpetrator was abusive; he or she could quite possibly continue to be abusive if this exchange were attempted in real life. In a real-life situation, the abuser might try to shut down the abused person, the abuser might simply exit the situation, or the abuser might try to harm the victim.

Role-playing the part of the negative Icon is somewhat like presenting a template where the client will perceive the missing elements. When role-playing the Icon, you present a blank or vague slate, and the client fills in the details. The important part of this role play is not the therapist and what he or she does within the role but the client and his or her effort to find their voice to express their internalized pain and sense of betrayal. The underlying principle to keep in mind is this: do not make an already very difficult exercise more difficult. As a therapist playing the role of the Icon, do not presume that you must be a strong and stubborn perpetrator. The perpetrator in this role play is not battling to win the day in the role play. If the role play is conceptualized as a win/loss scenario, then of course it is the client who should triumph. The client's efforts to assert his or her true self, should finally be heard. If you err in the portrayal of the abuser, err in the direction of being overwhelmed with guilt and now being apologetic. It is important to remember that you are dealing with, quite possibly, a traumatized victim who has deeply hidden but secretly denied fears of this type of confrontation. You as therapist, are trying to energize the quashed part of the person to stand up and face the Icon held within. The purpose of the exercise is to allow the anger and sadness in the victim to release. Remember, any movement by the client that expresses unresolved feelings towards the Icon is positive and therapeutic.

▶ Play the part with a soft voice

Play the part of the perpetrator from a bewildered and lost perspective, using themes of ignorance ("I didn't realize it was so bad, that it would hurt you so much"); self-centeredness ("I wasn't thinking of you; I was only thinking of my needs"); and personal confusion ("I was a pretty mixed-up person"). If the client insists on a more abusive adversary for the role, then suggest doing that later, when he or she has found their voice. In certain circumstances, they can be prepared to take on the actual person later, in real life, although this may not be recommended, as there may be a potential for harm.

▶ A Comment on Other Group Members Playing the Abuser

In the traditional psychodrama, developed originally by Jacob Moreno in France and the United States during the early 1900s, he used others in the group to play the part of the adversary. Often, he would use the role-reversal technique when couples attended with their marital problems. Playing the part of the person who hurt you in the marital relationship was encouraged, as it offered insight. It allowed one to gain an understanding of the problem from the perspective of the person on the other side. The problems Moreno addressed and the examples he cited were not as devastating as those being addressed in this approach.

In Iconic therapy, role reversal is never used in the group-therapy program. Only therapists play the part of the adversary in the role play. To play the part of the sex abuser, the abandoning parent, the loved one lost to suicide, or the murderer is too overwhelming for victims of these horrible events. Generally, group members, especially those who have been abused themselves, are not in a position to do this, even if they have worked through their issues. This is why it is important to have a skilled therapist take the part of the adversary. The sex-abuser part, for example, should be played by a sensitive and skilled therapist, who presents the abuser as somewhat remorseful and possibly abused himself. As well, if the role play does not work, it is best to leave the responsibility for its failure with the therapist rather than with another group member who is continuing to work through his or her own personal issues.

The same principles apply to domestic violence. When the extreme violence within this scenario is portrayed in role play, it can and should bring strong emotions in the client to the surface, especially anger. However, to be therapeutic, the person playing the part of the domestic violence abuser must present in a controlled and contrite manner, with just enough denial and blindness to set the stage for the client's release of anger. This is too much to ask another group member who has suffered and not healed from their own abuse.

For those who have suffered trauma as a consequence of the murder or suicide of a loved one, the role play where they would speak to the lost loved one is difficult enough. To contemplate having your client experience the pain suffered by their lost loved one, through a role-reversal scenario, would be close to unconscionable, and should be avoided.

It is important that the therapist have an understanding of how to play the adversary, the abusive person in a number of different scenarios. Examples of these will be presented below.

Role Plays for the Therapist

▶ Role-playing the part of the abandoning or dysfunctional parent

The hurt and psychic pain caused by the abandoning or dysfunctional parent is often presented in the therapeutic setting. To complicate the matter, the client may not realize the long-lasting impact of this type of experience. Even though the abuse may have been pervasive during one's youth, often the client has not been able to see it from any other perspective but from within the family setting. From that vantage point, the abuse is all that is known and the client is often not in a position to understand its full impact. As well, the client may have coped with the difficult circumstances by minimizing or denying the impact of the abuse, as to confront it directly would have risked survival. The same strategy is generally continued in therapy where they will report that the abuse was not that bad and/or that they have come to terms with it.

Let us presume that the therapist is presented with a client whose initial concerns is his anger for his wife and daughter. Through the interview, examples of the expression of this anger would be revealed. Then the session would turn to the client's personal history. ("I would like to take a personal history to get to know you.") Eventually the nature of the client's relationship with his parents would be discussed. It would then be learned that the client and his father struggled in their relationship and that the father had been abusive towards his son (the client). After completing the personal history the conversation would then return to a more detailed discussion regarding the nature of the abuse at the hands of the father (the core problem). The client would agree that he has never had the opportunity to fully express anger or sadness regarding abusive events that occurred between him and his father. Therapist and client would then have a discussion about what the client should say in the role play with the father, if he the client, were to be completely honest. Both would agree that a role play might help to release repressed thoughts, feelings, and emotions. Finally the moment has come when the therapist senses that the client is willing to take on the role-play exercise in accordance with his (the client's) belief that it might be beneficial.

The psychologist would begin.

| Therapist: | Let's do the role play with the father. The purpose of this exercise is to release unresolved anger for your father. Presently, this anger interferes with your relationship with your wife and daughter. I will speak for your father, and I will start. |
| Therapist: | [As father] Son, I understand you want to talk to me. What is it that you want to say? [A totally neutral beginning allows the son to take the initiative, to take control of the situation, and to take responsibility for changing how he relates to the father Icon.] |

Son:	Dad, I just want to say how hurtful it was when you would laugh at me and say I was stupid.
Therapist:	Son, I was not being serious; I was only kidding. That was my way of being funny.
Son:	Well, Dad, I want you to know that it hurt my feelings; it hurt me deeply to be called stupid so often. How would you feel if I called you stupid? I hated when you did that to me, and it made me very angry—anger I could never tell you about.

More dialogue occurs, possibly with the son raising specific examples of abuse. Eventually the father apologizes.

Therapist:	Son, I didn't realize what I was saying was so hurtful. I am sorry. I hope you can forgive me.

On paper, this type of exchange appears simplistic and not particularly consequential. However, in the therapeutic situation, the client, who most likely has been continually triggered in everyday life, to re-experience in some form these feelings of fear and anger, is now able to release these same emotions in the symbolic exchange with the perpetrator. Finally, these emotions will be placed on the perpetrator, where they belong. It will be a very important and therapeutic event. Exchanges as simple as these are very healing.

▶ Role-playing the part of the sexual abuser

Playing the part of the sexual abuser is also fairly straightforward once you are aware of the underlying principles. The psychologist or counsellor needs to have an understanding of what motivated the actions of the person who inflicted the pain, the sexual abuser. In most instances, the sexual abuser was motivated primarily by selfish and self-centered needs. Often the client will ask, "Why did you do it?", or "How could you do that to a five-year-old girl?" Here is an example of dialogue to use for the sexual abuser's responses in the role play, a role play that would have occurred after the disclosure exercise has been completed. The client has finally revealed his or her true emotions. He or she is now in a position to ask questions and express feelings that have haunted him or her for so long. The words used by the therapist (playing the abuser) are spoken softly in an effort to serve as a template for the actual abuser and to further encourage the client's release of deeply seated emotions. The therapist begins as follows:

Therapist: Let's do the role play with the sexual abuser. The purpose of the exercise is to release toxic emotions that include fear and anger on to the perpetrator. It is these emotions that leak into your everyday life and cause you to be anxious and angry. I will begin.

[As sexual abuser] You may not remember me. I was your babysitter when you were five years old. I am in AA now and trying to make amends for all my wrongdoings. If I hurt you, I want to say sorry, and if you have anything to say to me, I will listen and hear you. [This is an example of a gentle introduction to the role play.]

Client: You hurt me when you did what you did. I hated you when you did that. How could you do that? Why did you do it—why did you sexually touch me like that?

Therapist: I am sorry you were hurt so badly. I want you to know that I did it for entirely selfish reasons. I wanted pleasure, and I could get it from you.

Client: You wanted pleasure from a child? How could you not know how it would hurt me?

234

Therapist:	I wanted to have a sense of control and power in my life, and I could get that in my relationship with you. It wasn't really about you at all. It was entirely about me.
Client:	You're sick. What is wrong with you? Did you ever think of the damage you were doing?
Therapist:	I wasn't thinking that it would cause you pain or suffering. I just didn't think about it that way. I was only thinking about me. I was entirely lost in my own need for pleasure, power, and closeness. It wasn't about you at all.
Client:	It had an awful impact on me ... It ruined my sexual life ... I was always scared and frightened after that ... How could you do such a horrible thing? [At this point the client might bring up some examples of the impact of the abuse, which have already been discussed following disclosure. The client is free to say whatever she or he has to say; the true voice is finally released.]

Often, as part of the role play, the Icon (as played by the therapist) will apologize and ask for forgiveness. Regarding sexual abuse, this type of dialogue may be used:

I hoped you would have forgotten all that. I didn't realize it was so harmful. I guess I should have but I didn't. I'm sorry for the pain I caused. Could you ever forgive me?

About half the time, the victims of tragedy will not be able to forgive the perpetrator of such injustice. The therapist does not take a position on this point. That remains the prerogative of the client whose pain and suffering have often been long and extreme. It is not wise for the therapist to encourage forgiveness or to proffer opinions about the benefits of forgiveness at this stage. Sometimes, in a later role play with the perpetrator, the client may forgive him or her. It is best left open, and the final decision is always left with the client.

Another group member can be a helper, or *shadow*, who stands or sits next to the group member doing the role play and whispers things that could be said. It is my preference to have a co-therapist do this part, if it is required, as another group member may encourage words and phrases that do not fit for the victim. However, generally, the helper or shadow is not needed. It is ideal if the participant can do this on their own.

Therapists, please remember that the primary purpose of the role play is for the victim to find their voice and to express their unique sense of betrayal, anger, loss, and pain. As the clients move through this exercise (and following its completion), they will begin to understand more clearly the nature of the perpetrator. Where before they perceived an undefinable monster capable of anything, they now may have a moment when they understand that the perpetrator himself had problems. Even though they always suspected at a cognitive level that the perpetrator had problems, now at a deeper and more emotional level, they come to understand that the perpetrator was the damaged one, while they were innocent and undamaged before the abuse. With the successful completion of this role play, they begin to see themselves as healthier than before and empowered, now more capable of leaving the abuse and the abuser behind. As well, any misconception that they were somehow responsible for what occurred will leave them

▶ Role-playing the victim of suicide

If the primary trauma is the suicide of a loved one, then the "Goodbye" Role Play is often needed. The underlying purpose of this role play is to allow the client a final conversation with their lost loved one. As in the previous two examples, at least one counselling session (individual or group therapy) will be required for the client to disclose and discuss the occurrence of the suicide. However, with traumatic events of this severity, often more sessions of therapy are required to complete the disclosure and then to contemplate what should be said if a final conversation with the lost loved one could be arranged. Once the disclosure and the contemplation of what should be said have been completed, then the client will be in a position to consider taking on the role play.

Playing the part of the deceased loved one requires a very sensitive effort, wherein the love the deceased person carries for those left behind is expressed by the therapist. It would begin gently, with the therapist playing the part of the deceased person, setting up the role play as follows:

Therapist: The purpose of this exercise is to allow you to have a final conversation with … This will give you the opportunity to say words never said and express feelings that still linger within you, feelings that prevent you from moving forward. I will start.

              [As the lost loved one] They have let me return from the other side to speak with you one more time. What is it that you wanted to say to me? [This simple beginning statement opens the door for the client to release whatever it is that remains to be said. Often, the client will struggle to say the following.]

Client: I just miss you so much. Why did you do it? Why did you take your own life? Didn't you know I loved you so much? I'm angry at you for that.

Therapist:	I was just so lost in my problems I couldn't see a way out. I just thought everyone would be better off without me. I'm sorry now I did it. [This response again comes from the perspective of the suicided person, overwhelmed with emotions at the time of his or her death.]
Therapist:	[And later, from the deceased person] Please, do not grieve my death forever. You have your own life and special people to love. Thank you for being a very special person in my life. Thank you for loving me.

Of course, individual clients handle the suicide of family members in different ways. For many, it is a haunting and devastating experience that lingers within for years. Even though this exercise at a surface level appears to be going beyond what is needed, I can assure you that it does offer relief from a deep sense of dread and loss, and it will free your client to take on their on-going responsibilities of everyday life. When I play the part of the lost loved one, a person lost through murder, suicide or some other form of sudden death, I am often very moved. The emotions are so powerful that therapist and client together share deep levels of loss, sadness and regret. However, once these feelings are expressed, there is a sense of release, renewal and redemption.

▶ Role-playing the murderer

Losing a loved one to murder is another horrible event. For those of you who have never experienced such a thing or do not know anyone who has, the thought of losing a loved one in this fashion is beyond comprehension. Nevertheless, horrible events do occur in life, and as therapists, it is our duty and obligation to assist those left behind. In Iconic therapy, this is one of the most difficult role plays.

Role-playing the part of the murderer is an almost unconscionable option for most therapists and seldom used in most therapeutic relationships. However, there is more need for this type of treatment than you would expect as there are many clients who suffer from the loss of their loved ones to such a tragedy, a tragedy that carries with it an extremely damaging psychological aftermath.

Role plays with the murderer were successfully used with those damaged individuals that I worked with in the prison setting. It is a difficult therapeutic task, especially the effort required to encourage the client to take it on. Often, as one would expect, the client's anger and fear are very intense. This type of role play should only be used by a highly skilled and experienced therapist.

Again, the perpetrator is portrayed with selfish motives. For the therapist playing the part of the murderer, it is recommended that the opening line expresses a willingness to listen:

Therapist:	We will now do the role play where you speak to the person who ended the life of your … The purpose of this exercise is to provide for you the opportunity to express your thoughts and feelings regarding what happened. It is these feelings that interfere with your everyday decisions and your efforts to move forward. I will start.
	[As the murderer] They said you wanted to talk to me about what happened. I am willing to listen to whatever it is you wanted to say. [This type of opening allows the client to say what should be said without any particular direction being offered, thus allowing the client the opportunity to reveal his or her true self. The client might say the following:]
Client:	I hate you for what you did. How could you do such a thing?

Therapist:	I am so damaged as a person. I came to believe that violence was the only way when I didn't get what I wanted. I am not capable of remorse in the way you know it.
Client:	It was so terrible what you did. I can't understand why you would do such a horrible thing.
Therapist:	I was lost in my efforts to get control of my life. When I'm angry, I get lost in a rage. [The psychologist playing the part of the murderer does not portray the murderer as defensive or as justifying his actions, but rather like a murderer who has obtained some insight into his own behavior.]

When you speak in the role play, as the therapist, your primary goal is to have the client find their voice—the voice that will shape and deliver emotions in words that are finally addressed directly to the (symbolic) perpetrator. Your comments, speaking as the murderer, should be brief. You are the template, and the client will project their image of the murderer onto the template you present. You are the vessel into which will be poured the toxic anger and rage of your client. It is the client who has the lead part. It is the client who stands to become the empowered one in this effort.

If the client does begin to lose control, it is the responsibility of the therapist to bring the role play to a halt. This is easily done by merely saying, "We have to stop now; it is important that you have more control of your emotions." I have completed over 500 role plays involving a variety of scenarios, and I have drawn them to a halt less than five times. Rarely will the anger get to the point where you sense that the victim will strike you. I have never been struck by a client during a role play.

When a client enters treatment and begins the healing journey, it is extremely difficult for him or her to understand the impact of their suffering, let alone the motives of the person who brought on that suffering. When a client has lost a loved one to murder or suicide, they have also become a victim. Horrible events of this nature have the power not only to destroy the lost loved one but also, from a psychological perspective, their family members as well.

▶ Role-playing the person who supported the injustice

Often, as part of the disclosure, the client will reveal that she or he told their story to their mother or another respected and trusted person who was in a position to help (e.g., teacher, social worker, police officer, etc.). This person failed to act responsibly and the abuse continued, reinforcing the client's errors in thinking and Iconic echo (e.g., "You really did deserve it"). In my experience, especially in the sexual-abuse scenario, it is often the mother who has failed to help. For the role play, ideally a female therapist will play the part of the mother who has been perceived as supporting the abuse. (This is not essential, however; in most cases the role play works with either gender playing the mother.)

The primary theme in this role play is generally betrayal, but it can vary. Often the client in this role play will be addressing betrayal issues, as follows. The therapist speaking for the mother will begin this way:

Therapist: We will now do the role play with your mother. This will allow you to speak the words and express those feeling that have held you back. It is these feelings that now interfere with your everyday life and prevent you from moving forward. I will start.

[As the mother] I know you wanted to talk to me, your mom, about something. What is it?

241

Client: It is about when my stepfather sexually abused me. You knew it happened, and you didn't do anything. You stayed with him after he sexually abused me [or physically abused me, etc.]. You asked me not to report it when I should have. You didn't believe me and called me a liar.

The person playing the part of the mother often will offer a remark as follows, to set up the template to which the client can relate. These remarks vary in accordance with how the victim of the abuse recalled (during the disclosure exercise) what occurred:

Therapist: I didn't know you were being abused. I didn't realize it was that bad. I was abused myself, and I never dealt with my abuse. Dealing with yours was too hard, so all I could do was ignore it.

Generally, the unhelpful-mother template offers the following motivation, which may assist the client in gaining insight into the larger dynamic that allowed the abuse cycle to continue from one generation to the next. The unhelpful-mother role player will offer some insight into her betrayal:

Therapist: I was too afraid to do anything. I was filled with my own problems and they prevented me from being a protective and nurturing mother.

[The following sentences are grouped together for the sake of brevity. In the actual role play they would be sprinkled throughout the exchange between client and therapist.]

242

My inaction wasn't about you; it was about me and my weakness and my own abuse.

Although I will never be strong enough or honest enough in real life to apologize for my inability to help you, in this situation, in this exercise, let me say that deep in my heart, I do feel that I let you down when you need me the most.

I hope you can forgive me.

This role play can be preceded and supplemented with journaling by the candidate. If a client feels overwhelmed by the thought of any of the role plays suggested, it is often very helpful to have them write what should be said and bring the written material as a script to work from.

In this case, the abuser is of a secondary nature. When the primary abuser is perceived as extremely powerful, or abusive and loving at the same time, the client will often focus on the secondary abuser as responsible for what occurred. With this role play, this understandable confusion regarding the responsibilities of the secondary abuser will sort itself out.

The Therapist Has to Be Open to Allow the Suffering of the Client

The sexual-abuse experience is one that is frequently dealt with in Iconic therapy. In my efforts to mentor young psychologists and counsellors, I have learned that many hope that they will not meet clients who suffer certain types of problems, especially those of a sexual nature. They find this particular problem difficult and embarrassing to address. As well, many clients who have successfully completed the Iconic therapy program have told me that they attended other therapists who, after hearing about their sexual abuse, avoided discussing it in any depth. Many counsellors, psychologists and psychiatrists struggle with clients who have experienced sexual abuse. Often care givers have been abused themselves and have not dealt with their personal abuse. As well, sex is a difficult topic for many and often carries shame-based errors in thinking. If you are one of those psychologists, psychiatrists or caregivers who avoid the topic, you must realize that you will be letting down your abused clients and yourself when you are not present as the concerned and trusting witness to their disclosures. Your resistance to being a witness to their pain may encourage your clients to continue to carry shame that is not theirs to carry. Read the difficult passages shared by victims in this book and prepare yourself to hear difficult disclosures. Get treatment yourself, so you can be there for those who need you to play your part in the difficult but therapeutic role play.

As psychologists, psychiatrists, social workers, counsellors, caregivers, and healers, it is our responsibility to be there for our clients. We need to present with an approach that we know will help them through the pain they have endured and are still enduring.

When you take your client into a role play, you will experience moments when you, as the therapist, playing the part of the abuser, become that abuser in the mind of your client. Finally, the emotions your client so desperately wants to release have a forum and a modality for that release. Once those emotions (often anger, sadness, guilt, and shame) are expressed in the role-play exercise, the problems of your client shift significantly, and the underlying dynamic that supported a multitude of errors in thinking is diminished.

When you have guided your clients through the difficult disclosure and role-play exercises, you will have taken them on a healing journey that they could not have done alone. Your efforts will have allowed them to finally release very toxic, soul-destroying emotions and cognitions. For your anticipated future successes, I congratulate you! Please use the special relationship you have with your clients, and the power of this approach, with sensitivity, respect, and love for those who ask for your help.

The exercises that follow the role play are fairly straightforward so I will not expand on them in this appendix. It will be sufficient for you to read the main body of this text to familiarize yourself with the implementation of that aspect of this type of therapy.

APPENDIX 2

Supporting Data for the
Courage of Women Program

The Aggression Test and the Rosenberg Self-Esteem Test were administered to 86 participants in the Courage of Women program prior to their entering and after they left (pre- and post-testing). The results are reported below and support the view that the program had a positive impact upon those taking part.

The Aggression Test has five scales of aggression: physical, verbal, anger, hostility, and indirect hostility, which are summed to give an overall measure of aggression. The Rosenberg Self-Esteem scale has one self-esteem measure.[10]

---

[10] The reader is reminded that these women participated in a number of programs while incarcerated. It is difficult to discern if this particular program caused the change or whether the change was brought about by other factors. Their testimonials suggest it is the program. This possibility could be assessed with a control group. Women who attended other programs while not attending the Courage of Women could be compared with those who attended Courage of Women and the other programs.

Table 1. *Entering and exit scores for the woman attending the Courage of Women program*

Mean	Entering Score	Mean Exiting Score	t-score	p
Physical aggression	22.34	21.03	0.97	.168
Verbal aggression	15.10	13.49	2.42	.008*
Anger	21.00	18.38	2.80	.002*
Hostility	25.13	22.22	2.84	.003*
Indirect hostility	15.81	14.36	2.17	.016*
Aggression	99.17	87.80	3.09	.001*
Rosenberg self-esteem	14.89	19.04	5.85	.001*

*The scores on these scales were significantly different when the pre- and post-test scores were compared. As noted in the above table, the overall aggression score was significantly reduced. Of the five underlying scores, four were also significantly different, signifying that not only were the participants feeling less hostile but also that their proclivity to act out aggression was significantly reduced.

The Rosenburg self-esteem measures also showed very positive results. The women's self-esteem, as measured by this test, improved significantly.

Also, as part of the data collection, the women were asked to write personal comments regarding the impact of the treatment program. These comments were very supportive in nature and suggest that the improvement in self-esteem and reduction in hostility are most likely a function of this particular program.

Some comments made after one week

I feel better about myself, more self-confidence.

I wish I found out about the program sooner; I think it could have helped me a lot.

I'm able to be more honest with myself as well as others.

Kinda not ashamed of myself anymore; feel more confident.

I see the pattern of my lifestyle and realize what I need to do to change that pattern.

It is a relief knowing that I am not the only one this happened to. I'm not alone.

I am taking control of my life so my kids don't go through what I did.

I have more courage to speak up.

The first time I ever talked about my abuse was when I was in Courage of Women.

Now that I see I am not the only woman to have gone through the emotions and the pain, I am comfortable talking about my abuse in and out of the group.

Some comments made after one month

I understand why I made some of the decisions that I have made in my life ...

I have more hope for the future ...

I am more open and willing to talk about feelings to family/friends ...

I'm not scared about what others think anymore.

It's all good ...

I know that if I want to make changes in my life, I have to take action ...

I have a brighter outlook, higher self-confidence.

I stood up for myself for the first time the other day, and I felt so great after. I never had the courage to do that before in my life.

I realize I am a confident and powerful woman.

Joining Courage was the smartest thing I have ever done in my life.

A total of 59 women responded to the following questions after one month in attendance, comprised of eight group-therapy sessions. *Note*: SA=Strongly Agree, A=Agree, NC=No Change, D=Disagree, SD=Strongly Disagree, IN=Incomplete. There is a clear impression that most in the program felt that they had benefited.

Table 2. *Post-Therapy Responses*

Question	SA	A	NC	D	SD	IN
This group has allowed me to develop a more positive view of men.	25%	32%	43%	0%	0%	0%
The role play(s) did not help me get over my sexual abuse.	0%	0%	18%	21%	25%	43%

When back in the community, I will be the kind of person who can stand as a spokesperson against abuse in the community.	29%	39%	21%	0%	11%	0%
My ability to trust in a relationship has improved.	18%	25%	46%	11%	0%	0%
My temptation to drink and use drugs is less than before.	21%	36%	25%	18%	0%	0%

Note: The correctional officers often commented that once the Courage of Women program had been implemented, the number of fights and verbal altercations occurring on the women's units diminished significantly. The female inmates became more cooperative with each other and with the correctional officers.

Printed in the United States
By Bookmasters